*Let Go Courageously and Live with Love*
*Transform Your Life with Feng Shui*

# LET GO **COURAGEOUSLY** AND

# *Live with Love*

## TRANSFORM YOUR LIFE
## WITH FENG SHUI

# LAURA STALEY

Cherish Your World Publishing
P.O. Box 14201
Columbus, Ohio 43214
cherishyourworld.com

987654321

First Edition
Printed in the United States of America

This edition is printed on acid-free paper that meets the American National Standards Institute Z39.48 Standard.
This book is printed on 30% postconsumer recycled paper.

*Designed by Kim Dhuyvetter*

THE LIBRARY OF CONGRESS CATALOGUES THIS BOOK AS FOLLOWS:
ISBN: 978-0-9974584-0-4
LCCN: 2016907659
1. Feng Shui.  2. Personal Development.  3. Inspirational.

Dedicated to Kate

Because I knew you, I've been changed for good.

# CONTENTS

# INTRODUCTION

I t's a joy to share with you these short stories of my journey
with my two great passions: family life and feng shui.
During the past 15 years, I've lived in three homes, and each
of them has needed varying degrees of transformation. My
gateway into the study and practice of feng shui came after a
life-altering flood of the finished basement of my first home.
Although it looked like a muddy and messy challenge, the
flood gave birth to my career as a feng shui consultant and my
life purpose.

Learning to live with love and let go with courage has
involved deep and sometimes painful self-discovery. In the
process, I have had to create a core love of myself. Seeing
that I lived with unloved belongings helped me realize that I
hadn't been loving myself or even knowing who I truly was.
When I read that I could *live with belongings I loved,* this idea
awakened me and felt so right. Thus, the wisdom of feng shui
has helped to guide me in needed directions. Letting go, while
challenging, has been a key element of transforming my life,
just as it was essential to transforming my home.

I've let go of once-beloved possessions (and the never-
beloved ones, too) that weren't going to be part of my life as
I went forward. I've let go of patterns in my life that were not
serving me. I've let go of two homes that I'd loved and that
had made me feel deeply safe and supported. I've let go of
contact with family members with whom I was experiencing toxic patterns—and later resumed some contact when a
deep healing took place. I've let go of beloved pets who loved
me unconditionally. I've let go of a husband and a marriage,
and my dreams of what that would be in my later years. I've

watched both my children leave my home under very different circumstances. I've let go of the security I once had about
what my life was and how it was going to unfold.

These essays flow out of these experiences. Most of the
essays conclude with a list of ideas you can consider for your
home and life. The essays span the time period from my initial
discovery of feng shui through 11 years of being a consultant,
educator, and speaker. They are organized chronologically for
those of you who enjoy reading a book from beginning to end;
you may instead want to open the book to those essay titles
that most resonate with your life right now. A handful of the
essays address areas of the home you may choose to clear and
enhance. Several essays focus on the importance of clearing our
minds of thoughts or beliefs that disempower us and choosing
ones that uplift us. Still other essays focus on the safety and
comfort of belongings. All of the essays embrace the transfor-
mational power of feng shui and the ways that integrating these
ideas into your life can create positive change.

Simple and sometimes subtle feng shui ideas, when imple-
mented, have had powerful and positive effects for my clients.
The title of this book, *Let Go Courageously and Live with Love:
Transform Your Life with Feng Shui*, summarizes the main
message of this ancient wisdom. Let everything go that you
do not need, including thoughts and relationships that have
negative effects on your life. Live with people you love, pets
you adore (if pets bring you joy), and belongings you treasure.
Learning about feng shui can be a process that shapes who
you are and how you experience your life and your home.

You can unveil your most deeply held dreams and get rid
of ones that were given to you by others or expected of you.
You can take similar actions with your belongings. Most of

the time you know when something is only taking up space, standing in your way, or even causing negative thoughts and feelings.

I hope these essays help you discover what you love and what you don't, and give you ideas about ways you can live with love. As you read these essays, be inspired by the ideas that will work for your life and your living space. Know that your home and life tell a story of challenges and dreams, heartaches and hearts' desires. You can transform your home and life through courageously letting go of what no longer inspires you and living with love. Read on, my friends!

## FROM A FLOOD TO FENG SHUI
*Birthing a Purpose and a Passion*

It's Valentine's evening and my husband and I are watching a romantic comedy that I no longer remember because the experience that unfolds creates a shredded document in my brain's file folder. A personal drama silently sneaks in while we cuddle on the couch in the family room of our finished basement. Our four-year-old daughter and 18-month-old son sleep soundly as water seeps into our utility room. Up through a drain, it flows from a convergence of rain, melted snow, and an improperly installed 60-year-old sewer pipe. Walking toward the bathroom, I step onto a squishy carpet, soaking my socks. I call to my husband.

As a couple we react quite differently. My husband minimizes the potential for damage, thinking that the water will stop and recede. I hysterically overreact; I imagine a deep swimming pool of water causing the basement walls to cave in, all our belongings to drown, and our home to implode. We do nothing but yell at each other.

"THE WATER WILL STOP FLOWING!"

"SAVE THE STUFF BEFORE OUR HOME IMPLODES!"

The water, meanwhile, wells forth, indifferent to our argument. It soaks the entire carpet in every inch of our downstairs living space. Our son cries out for his nighttime breastfeeding. With ice-cold wet feet, I creep upstairs.

I return to my husband's side, wide awake and calmer. I see that the unrelenting rise of water has finally shifted his attention to action. He's in grab-and-go mode. Finally united in focus, we grip as many items as we can from the family room, guest room/office, storage room, and utility room, and then we wade through the icy water, drag them up the stairs and through the breezeway, and dump them onto the garage floor.

My brother and sister-in-law, after my desperate midnight phone call, generously arrive to help us. They carry out boxes, toys, chairs, and lamps, but so much remains below, unsalvageable, drowning in the ice-cold blackness that is almost knee-high. Hours later, we hug one another, our bodies drained and our faces sad, as we say goodbye. They keep saying how sorry they are and asking if we are sure there isn't something more they can do. We thank them many times through a haze of weary defeat. We assure them, "It is just stuff. No one is hurt. Everyone is okay. We'll be okay."

I close the garage door as their car headlights retreat into the rainy, cold night. Turning around, I see my husband weeping. Having only seen him cry one other time, I am broken open by this sight. We hold each other and shake with sobs. At 4 a.m., we collapse into bed.

Much of my life, I have known that out of challenging situations good things can be found. I look for the silver lining like a persistent treasurer hunter. In the days that follow, I search diligently for the purpose of this heartbreaking experience. Fortunately, the answers arrive within weeks.

A month later, while I am visiting my husband's family in Florida, my beloved sister-in-law unknowingly becomes my muse. As we walk through her neighborhood on a sunny afternoon, she shares excitedly about feng shui. Curious and clueless, I take the book she hands me when we arrive back at her home. I hold it: Terah Kathryn Collins' *The Western Guide to*

*Feng Shui: Room by Room.* I open it to the page titled "Live with What You Love." Initially bewildered, I reject this idea; after all, it's just stuff. But I am intrigued by the idea, and I read about how you can love your belongings, and your home can be an expression of your tastes and preferences. I read most of the book on the plane ride back to Columbus.

Walking back into our home and standing in our dining room, I am hit by a wave of profound awakening. It's as if I am seeing my belongings for the first time. As my eyes take in the decor of our home, I see hand-me-downs everywhere. I notice that I don't like most of them. A deeper realization arises: *I'm living a hand-me-down life!* I don't dislike my life, yet in this moment existential questions buzz around me. Who the heck am I? Why am I here? What am I really here to do and be? Where am I in this home? Who am I?

There certainly are choices I made that came from the core of me, such as dissolving my first marriage, marrying a second time, and becoming a mother. Yet I reflect on so many choices that follow a script crafted to meet other people's expectations. From this perspective, I see an unhappy story of a person living an imposter's life. This house and its contents push against me. Like a powerful psychic, our home speaks a truth I now hear: My life isn't fully my own.

Uplifted by the permission to live with what I love, I wake up from a sleepwalking life into an uncomfortable reality with an action plan for both outer changes and inner reflection. I can do this! I begin a process of discovering who I am and what I love underneath layers of demeaning messages, which shaped my lack of worth. Over the next several months, I carry even more things out of our home. I no longer ever have to live with belongings I dislike or loathe.

I remove dishes selected by my mom and sister from my first marriage, clothes that my mom had altered to fit me, love letters from guys I dated years ago, furniture from dead family members, and artwork that gives me the creeps. I box and bag so many disliked items. Driving them in loads to donate to charities or sell at consignment shops, I liberate our home from old energy of sadness, guilt, obligation, humiliation, fear, and anger. I realize that several items seem harmless, functional, and even pretty to the unsuspecting eye, but in context, these items are enmeshed with nightmarish memories for me. I am so empowered and relieved to escort them off of our property.

While the new carpet settles onto the concrete floor of our now clean and dry basement, patterns of behavior that clung to me for years, like black mold on caulking between the tiles in an old shower stall, begin to dissolve. I begin to discover my true desires and new ways of loving my home and loving my life.

I take my time. Initially we live with lots of empty spaces and walls. For the first time in my life, rooms exist for me to just breathe and be. I find a sense of safety, of freedom. I find the ability to speak my truth, and a career path that integrates my passion and wisdom. I find a way to serve that helps others to express themselves through their surroundings, a way to guide others to fulfill their dreams. Over time a happy, peaceful, inspired self emerges alongside some new beloved belongings that I purchase because I love them and they reflect who I am. This flood, which had initially seemed so destructive, ultimately creates transformation and an enduring passion for the art and practice of feng shui.

Here are some suggestions to consider as you contemplate the idea of living with love:

- Look closely at your living space, working space, or both. What do you see? Is there a metaphor for some aspect of your life?

- Ask yourself: *What do I like best about my home? What do I like least? What do I like the best about my life? What do I like the least? Is there a connection between my physical space and some aspect of my life?*

- Consider that your home serves a purpose and so does your life. What are these purposes?

- If you are living through a challenging time, consider that transforming your physical space might serve as a pathway to stability and evolution. Challenges offer opportunities for reflection and growth. Often these storms, floods, or frustrating interpersonal dynamics push us to let go of something, someone, or some thought or feeling that no longer belongs in our lives. Can you take a moment to unclasp your hands?

- If you notice belongings in your living space that no longer align with who you are now, pick them up and carry them off your property. They have served their purpose in your life and now you can let them go, set them free.

## SINGING THE BEDROOM BLUES
*Envisioning Your Bedroom as a Haven*

After all the purging of hand-me-downs in the months following our Valentine's Day flood, I felt inspired to make other transformations in my home. I stood in our bedroom and thought to myself: *Let's make this room really peaceful. It could all be blue—that's a peaceful color.* I shared this with my husband and he agreed. He installed blue window blinds. We purchased powder-blue plush carpeting and painted the walls a slightly lighter shade of blue. Our bedspread has lots of blue in it, too. The room indeed is peaceful, and deep sleep has found its way into our routine. But now, several months later, I realize something's missing. In a moment of panic and disbelief, it hits me: Sleep is all that happens in this room!

I realize the pattering of two pairs of little feet now occupy our home, but the presence of children in our lives has rarely interrupted this domain of our marriage until now. Yet now, inside this monochromatic room, we experience a disconnection. Crabbiness and nitpicking have replaced loving looks and tender kisses in our interactions, both in and out of the room. When was the last time we drove away on a date? I open my beloved copy of *The Western Guide to Feng Shui: Room by Room* by Terah Kathryn Collins. I turn to the section on bedrooms and the chapter on the five elements. It is still four years before I will undergo formal training in feng shui, and I'm still learning.

My initial experiment enhancing my bedroom, I gather from my reading, has shoved away harmony and balance. I learn

that blues and greens are cool colors, which are not optimal in a
bedroom if one desires sensuality and conjugal relations. I also
realize that the wood element overpowers the entire room. I
read that when actual wooden items and wood's representatives
(such as the color blue) take over a physical space, over time the
people living there can experience stress, irritation, impatience,
and anxiety. These words resonate with my experience.

I also notice the ancestor photos—including the old-
fashioned, no-one-dare-smile framed family members—
staring from a corner of our bedroom. I look at them. These
*must* leave our bedroom. I find other areas in our home to
place some of these photos. Many find their way into photo
boxes as I realize I actually don't need stern, mean faces
watching me anywhere in our home.

Rather than tear out the carpeting or take down the
expensive window blinds, we choose to paint. My husband
and I work together to bring a lovely shade of cream, soft and
buttery, to our bedroom walls. It feels warmer and definitely
balances the woodwork and the remaining blue in the room. I
invest in a new quilt with pinks, reds, and creams, and purchase
reddish-pink throw pillows for our bed. On the wall vacated
by the ancestors, I place an artist's drawing of two cats with
dreamy smiles, faces that capture sated looks of bliss, joy, love,
and sweetness. The blue cloud lifts.

My husband and I engage in several heartfelt conversations
about the state of our union, the patterns of defending ourselves
from the irrational threat of the other, the soft unmet needs
that lie buried underneath the fierce fortress of "I'm fine," and
the disappearance of kind and gentle tactile contact. When I
feel as though I'm about to erupt, I learn to interrupt myself by
identifying exactly what I'm upset about; often it has nothing to

do with the current reality or with my husband. The issues that seem to be upsetting me are only false evidence appearing real, a whiff of something that reminds me of past trauma. Sometimes I need a hug, and I realize I can ask for this first rather than storming through the painful and more circuitous route of full-blown tantrum, seething silence, and tears of shame. My husband creates a practice of grounding himself in the room during a disagreement even though he so badly wants to leave. By staying, he chooses to listen, to gently hold me, and to talk out a resolution.

With the outer changes now supporting us as a couple, we find our way back to each other, to kindness and affection. We realize this fulfills a foundational need in both of us. Kissing, hand-holding, back rubbing, hugging, and greeting one another after being apart all weave their way back into our daily interactions. We hire a babysitter and schedule dates. In and out of our bedroom, we experience a healthier and more vibrant marriage.

Here are ideas to consider when you want to create a bedroom that is both sensuous and peaceful:

- Relocate all items that create obstacles to sleep and romantic interaction, if this is part of your life. This might include removing electronics, piles of bills, and workout equipment. If space is limited, look for ways to enclose or cover items that may interfere with sleep. Studies now show that the light from electronics tricks the brain to register daylight. Optimal sleep requires peace, darkness, and quiet.

- Strive for a balance of elements in your room. Warm colors in shades of purple, orange, and red represent the fire element, and brown, cream, and yellow bring in the elements of earth. Fire energy embodies emotions, and just the right amount can heat up the bedroom. Earth energy grounds and stabilizes. This element may be especially important if you have a really large bedroom with a high ceiling. Monochromatic bedrooms—all wood, all white, or all blue—stifle us and disconnect us from the richness and tapestry of life and ourselves. It's like being at the beach with only the sand or eating only iceberg lettuce as a salad.

- If possible, place your bed in the command position with a view of the door from the headboard, but not in the pathway of the door. This optimal placement allows the body to shift into a calm and relaxed state. If restorative sleep is elusive for you, this repositioning of the bed may be especially helpful.

- Some people hold thoughts and feelings on the inside, and others process thoughts and feelings on a megaphone. Find the sweet spot of sharing and listening respectfully and knowing that one point of view isn't the only valid point of view.

- Live true to your way of communicating love. In what ways do you enjoy being loved? In what ways do you demonstrate your love for others? For some, it's with kind words and listening with presence; others give and receive thoughtful gifts. Maybe you relish performing kind deeds and giving and receiving hugs. Some people love by creating time for fun adventures together. Most of us use a combination of ways for showing others we really do care. Live true to your preferred ways of expressing love and honor other people's ways of loving you.

SWEET SPOTS INSIDE THE CHAOS

*Living with Love and Young Children*

When the flood that started my feng shui journey happened in our home, my son was 18 months old and my daughter was four. So both of them swam in a fish bowl in which clearing clutter, organizing, arranging furniture and artwork, and rearranging were regular occurrences. Because I worked as a feng shui consultant, the many benefits of the practices and principles of feng shui became part of their experience growing up.

Loving our children is as easy as breathing, but parenting remains the hardest job in the world. As many parents have, I've worked diligently to understand child development and evolve my human skills, knowing that I needed to break free of my own messy upbringing. I often felt helpless and ill-equipped to manage the emotional chaos of small children. Often I threw my own tantrum or wept on the floor right next to them. I found that I had a lot of work to do to be the healthy and loving parent I knew I could be. I also found that by containing some of the physical chaos of my home, I could better manage my own strong feelings and respond to those of my children.

It is possible to find sweet spots of calm and order amid the rocking ride of parenting young children. Below I share some of the ideas that can make a difference for busy parents with young children. These ideas are inspired by many experiences with my own children, my clients and their children, and the spaces and places we all live, eat, sleep, and play.

## Special Time Switch-Off

If you have multiple children and parents in your family, consider having periods of time in which you bond with each of your children one on one through an activity that your child chooses, perhaps from a few options that you offer. This is something you can do on a small scale most days and on a larger scale once a month or at the frequency that best fits your family's needs and schedules. The benefits of special time include bonding in a fun and relaxed way and mitigating sibling squabbling.

At the scheduled time, usually on Sundays, my husband and I would take one child and play with that child one on one for a time, and then switch children. Our son usually loved being outside and active, while our daughter tended to love imaginative play.

On a day-to-day basis, with really small children, even 10 minutes of special time can be a pleasant addition to your day, especially when you can be present and engaged with your child during this time. This sometimes can happen when a baby brother or sister naps. While this time can be a challenge to fit into our busy lives, it's a practice that has many rewards. Breathe in these moments. It can become something everyone looks forward to.

In addition to building in special time on a daily basis, you can have an outing with one parent and child on a monthly basis, or whatever timeframe works for your family. We wrote this special time on the calendar and could show our children when they would get special time. Scheduling outings reinforces to the children that they are valued. As children get older, you can change the kinds of activities as you notice that their interests evolve and change.

In a family where there are more children than parents, it may be trickier to schedule this time, but it can still be doable when older children are at preschool or school, or when some children are with friends or other loved ones. Have a relaxed approach to finding and implementing this time, and do what works best for your family.

**The Donate-Keep Ritual**

The belongings of children seem to flow out into every space, nook, and cranny of our homes. This can become visually overwhelming and even a safety hazard. (If you've ever stepped on a Lego, you know exactly what I mean.) Containing the toys to certain rooms can seem impossible, let alone finding a child's bed amid all their treasures in a bedroom. If toys and kid stuff become overwhelming, it can be difficult for a child to find beloved toys or choose one activity. For some, this physical chaos becomes the new normal and they roll with it. For others, the physical chaos creates stress and anxiety. They may feel out of control and the physical world matches this experience. Find out where your children's sense of comfort is on this long continuum. Again, keep looking for the sweet spot of balance for you and your children. The practice of donate-keep can help.

Every six months or before a child's birthday, consider sitting with your children and helping them sort belongings into two piles: *donate* and *keep*. Explain to them that items in the donate pile can go to kids who have few or no toys, or who were affected by a fire or natural disaster in which their toys got destroyed. (Some children might be frightened by this idea; you can determine whether mentioning this would be helpful or upsetting.) Allow your child to decide which items go where. I suggest beginning this process with five-or six-year-olds; you know your own child and can tweak this accordingly.

I remember my son holding on to a plastic hammer he never played with; I wanted the decision about what to let go of to be his, so I didn't debate the issue with him. It went into the keep pile. Three months later, he voluntarily brought the hammer to me and told me he was done with it. "Donate it, Mommy."

For children younger than 5 or 6, you can gather and box up less used items. Keep them handy in case your child asks about them. If after six months these items aren't missed, then you can donate them or give them to friends with young children or those who are expecting.

It helps to model this behavior when you, too, are making decisions about what to keep and what to donate. Consider showing your children all the belongings you are choosing to release and those you know you will keep, or encouraging them to help you move items into piles or containers as you make these decisions.

### The "Good Night, Toys … Good Night, Books" Ritual

If a child's room seems too stimulating because it's filled with toys and books that distract him or her from going to sleep, play a game of putting everything to sleep and tucking the belongings in at night. You may drape a blanket over the bookshelf and say, "Good night books, sleep tight—see you in the morning." Several of my clients embraced and benefitted from this idea. You and your children may, too!

You can bring in containers for sorting toys and put the toys to bed. Work to calm the room down visually by tucking things away out of sight or under blankets. It can become a soothing ritual your child performs as he or she gets older.

If possible, relocate as many items as you can to a separate room so that your child's bedroom becomes a true place for *sleep*. I strongly encourage you to relocate TVs and other technology to other rooms in the house, especially if restful sleep is a challenge for your child.

### The Craft Cupboard

Consider creating a storage space for crafts that school-aged children can easily access.

I dedicated one entire cabinet next to the dining room for crafts; I still call it the craft cupboard. I placed plastic drawer containers on the shelves, each holding different types of items: play-clay, crayons, stickers, colored pencils, glue sticks, scissors, and paper. The kids had access to this cupboard and could get supplies out anytime they wanted to draw or make something with craft items. During the school years, this cabinet became the place to find supplies for school projects. My children easily returned all the supplies to this convenient cabinet, because they could reach it easily.

You or some of your family members may be visually cued. If this is the case, consider keeping items on open shelving units in full view or in clear containers. You can experiment and find out what works best for you and your children. This idea is meant to help restore order and keep mental clarity flowing, as well as creativity. When you cannot locate what you need and desire, it can be more challenging to create.

Each person has his or her own place on the continuum from preferring pristine order to liking to have items in the open, which some people might view as a disorderly mess. Distinguish what works for you and your family. You know your children best.

## The Multi-Purpose Dining Table

Many families use the dining room or kitchen table for many purposes, including eating, crafting, working, doing homework, and playing board games.

Whenever a room or table serves several purposes, it's important to be able to easily clear it for the next use. For example, meals ideally should take place on a table that's free of work, school papers, or bills, all which could distract family members from the purpose of eating and bonding with one another.

Eating together is such a special social ritual for nourishing our bodies, hearts, and souls. Some of my favorite memories are ones I spent eating, talking, and laughing at the dining room table during a meal. Of course, my favorite memories also include the times at that same table when I laughed with my daughter while helping her with homework or a paper she was writing.

To accommodate these multiple uses for your dining table, all of which are important in your home, work to keep the table and surrounding area (which might be a dining room in your home or a designated part of your kitchen) free and clear of objects not intended for mealtime, such as exercise equipment, "to-read" piles, TVs, and garden tools. Consider relocating these items to other areas of the home. You can create cabinets or shelves to store non-dining items between uses. When the dining area is clear and serene, it helps to make dining and digestion more peaceful.

## Treasure Boxes

I gave each child a long, large "treasure box" to hold meaningful keepsakes and mementos. Once a year, usually at the end of a school year, I sat with my children as we'd go through their treasure boxes and look for things they no longer wanted to keep.

I remember my son letting go of elementary school items. Once he was in middle school, he couldn't remember many kids from preschool and grade school. He easily let go of the cards and trinkets associated with those children.

This once-a-year ritual is especially important because otherwise, the box may get stuffed. I did not buy any more boxes. I told my kids the one box was it. As time passed, they found it easy to let go of items that no longer held meaning in their changing lives.

I especially remember sitting with my daughter a few weeks before she left for college and going piece by piece through her treasure box. We laughed looking at photos of her middle school friends and cried as she read letters. We opened a calendar I created during her first year of life with milestone stickers and notes I had written about her and how much her dad and I love her. She kept this calendar, a true treasure.

**Parent Treasure Box**

Have your own treasure box of the items you value most, both related and unrelated to your children. Be open to releasing old birthday cards, Christmas cards, and other mementos. Know and trust that in the years to come, you will continue to receive both birthday and Christmas cards from people who love you. Take photos if needed as a way to remember your favorite cards before you put them in the recycling bin. Otherwise, you might find that these items pile up so much that you cannot find the items that are truly meaningful to you.

You may find it difficult to let go of children's artwork, schoolwork, and homemade gifts. It may help you to remember that creating artwork often involves the joy of the process itself. With children, especially, there is often less attachment to the product and great joy inside the process of creating. Keep artwork up that inspires you and your children. If your children have graduated from high school, consider taking down the kindergartner finger paintings hanging in the living room, or choose just one, frame it, and store the rest. Again, take lots of photos if you need to, and keep your very favorite items for your treasure box. Let the rest go, trusting that you are making room for new memories that will come.

## The Wish List

Anytime you are in a store or out and about, have a pad of paper and pen in your purse and write down ideas your children share with you about things they would love to have. Tell them that the item is going on the wish list, and let them watch you write down the information about the item they would like. Next birthday or Christmas, choose an item on that list you think your child would still enjoy, and purchase it. You might notice some items are forgotten the moment after you write them down. Let those ones go, too.

This idea allows young children to be heard and validated for a desire they have in the moment. It empowers the imagination for both children and adults with our "bucket list" of dreams and aspirations.

## Secure Your Own Oxygen Mask First

I've grown to have deep compassion for parents, especially those who struggle to manage their stress and anger, and heal the wounds of their own childhood. Once I hit my daughter's bottom in a moment of rage. I don't even remember now what she had done; I'm certain she was only being a two-year-old. I know I terrified her; I terrified myself. I never did it again (although I continued to struggle with feelings of rage that seemed to come out of nowhere). At that moment, I knew that people who hit their kids rarely do it from a place of deep love and peace inside themselves. I also knew that I needed help responding in the best ways I could to the challenges of parenting. I now know why hospitals give parents numbers to call so they won't abuse their children. I know why parenting classes are mandatory for some people and why many organizations exist to help parents heal their own trauma or childhood wounds. Breaking the cycle takes commitment, persistence, and courage.

Keep in mind that the advice the flight attendants give to passengers with children applies to us in life too: We need to secure our own oxygen masks and then help our children with theirs. That is, we need to work to heal ourselves and to find strategies to best deal with young children. I encourage you to look outward for the people and resources that can help you to be the parent you want to be.

I had done a lot of healing before becoming pregnant, but it turned out that was only the tip of the iceberg. Inside the experience of parenting is where I discovered both my strengths and my trauma that had to heal. In addition to the work I did in counseling and various other modalities, I reached outward for other experts who could help me to be the parent I wanted to be. I cherish all the authors, preschool teachers, life coaches, mentors, clients, and therapists who shared wisdom that continues to resonate with my heart.

It is also important that on a day-to-day (and sometimes moment-by-moment) basis, you balance caring for your children with caring for yourself. Take the time you need to meet your own needs, whatever they may be.

## CINDERELLA'S PAIN AND THE RETURN
## OF SANITY
### *Creating a Healthy Experience of Cleaning*

On Saturday morning, my younger brother and I wake up before anyone else. We sneak to the family room and turn on the TV. Even though we know what's coming, the animated characters with silly voices beckon. Unfortunately, my parents' bedroom is much too close to the noise of our black-and-white boob tube. My mother appears in the doorway, already simmering. Entering the room where my brother and I sprawl on the floor playing with toys and watching Bugs Bunny cartoons, she yells, "Turn off the damn TV and go do your Saturday chores!"

My chores include scrubbing down both full bathrooms, cleaning my side of the room I share with my older sister, and ironing all the family's freshly laundered clothes. My brother and sister find activities outside our home and leave promptly. Left alone, isolated from others as witnesses and buffers, I scramble to get right to the list. While I'm in the bathroom cleaning, she blasts in. "Why aren't you done in here? You have your room to clean!" I never am doing what she thinks I should be doing. I am never doing things in the time frame she demands. I cannot split myself into five or ten selves to meet her insistence on simultaneous task delivery.

Finally in my room, I work consciously and steadily on dirt and dust removal. All the knick- knacks on my dresser get a wipe-down, as do the bookshelves and swimming trophies. I plug in the Hoover upright vacuum and get in every nook and cranny it will reach. Nothing is on the carpeting that I can see. I move the sweeper back and forth so many times that I can't imagine a tiny dust mite surviving the suction. As I tug on the cord to unplug the machine, she thunders in, her face contorted. "This room isn't clean! Do you think this room is clean? I see specks here and over there! What were you doing in here with all that time?" Then the cussing and the denigrating verbal tirade begin. I leave my body and my heart drops into a deep freezer. My mind goes numb as I watch her face deepen to crimson. The spittle from her mouth mixes with hateful words and seems to splatter all over the room like blood spurting from puncture wounds. Years later I learn that this type of explosion is called "annihilating rage." The phrase fits.

I grab the Hoover, plug it in, and flip the switch. I vacuum with rigor and pour all my terror and indescribable rage into the effort of sucking away the invisible specks she sees with her x-ray vision. Channeling a combination of fight/flight energy into the rhythmic back-and-forth of pushing a vacuum, I unknowingly create a sort of healthy choice for myself. The trauma in my body releases a tiny bit. At least in this moment, I'm not a deer in the headlights.

Years later, after I leave my parents' home, cleaning shows up as a ritual, a coping strategy. I discover that cleaning has become my body's attempt to release the thousands of stored-up shocks to my nervous system, the persistent traumatic stress of living with a mother who suffered with a heinous mental illness. When I'm scared, depressed, lonely, or stressed, I clean. It becomes part of the driven, out-of-balance person I become. It appears to be healthy, but it's an undistinguished way to cope. It shows up as a yellow flag signaling me about my possible off-kilter relationship to my environment, but I'm not quite ready to dig deeper. However, when I become a parent, my obsession with cleaning shifts from a mere yellow flag to something completely unhealthy.

As a mother of two young children, I work fervently to calm myself amid the emotional and physical chaos of this new reality. I obsess about cleaning. The scene in Mary Poppins with all the singing, finger snapping, and toys and clothes magically putting themselves away rewinds and plays again in my mind. I work to make cleaning up a group effort, a fun activity we all do together while singing songs: "Clean up, clean up, everybody, everywhere ..." I think I'm teaching my kids the joy of orderliness, but actually I'm working desperately to soothe myself. My fixation with tidiness consumes me.

I become obsessed with leaving the house clean before we go anywhere. I'm driven by a need to create peace and orderliness in my outer world with things I can actually move around, throw away, or pick up and put in a drawer. I think that if I can return to a tidy home after being away from my house, I will be less inclined toward even greater agitation. It makes transitions leaving from our home really challenging and perplexing for my kids, who do not understand my need to put everything away, vacuum, dust, and mop. I'm clearly running from the ghost of my mom's rage chasing me all around the house that my children now live in.

I know I won't yell at my kids about a clean house, and I don't. However, there are still multidimensional costs to my obsession with cleanliness. I live with what abuse creates in the nervous system as well as my whole being. I have inner agitation, angst, and night terrors. Some might call it post-traumatic stress disorder. Finally aware that I need help, I shift my attention away from the disorder in my physical space and turn to therapists, those skilled in resolving trauma. Fiercely committed to paying forward something healthy and finding inner sanity, I slowly break free from this out-of-control need to have a super-tidy home and its cost to my sanity. I recognize that I craved a deep sense of safety because I never was safe as a child. I had equated tidiness with emotional and physical safety. In reality, they are not connected. Keeping a clean room never stopped my mother's abuse. Nothing I did or didn't do stopped her abuse because her abuse was about her illness and not my existence or the orderliness of a physical space. I begin to find inner peace and resilience, and to heal the long-ago traumas.

Now that I am calm, aware, and at a distance from my trauma, I realize that on any given day, the state of my home ranges from tidy to messy. Some days a few dirty dishes remain in the sink before dinner, and toys remain scattered on the floor all night long. I discover the nuance of living with some mess and relaxing inside of it. Enjoying my kids becomes more important than frantically cleaning. I model a healthier relationship with both tidy and messy states and this shows my children a sense of balance and sanity.

My children, now teenagers, sometimes launder and fold their clothes. Sometimes they load the dishwasher and wipe counters. Sometimes they don't, and my husband and I step in. It ebbs and flows. My son and daughter have the freedom to create the physical chaos of clothes strewn on the floor of their rooms and the feelings associated with clean and organized surroundings when they're encouraged or when they choose. At this point on the parenting journey, I trust them to find their own comfort level with cleanliness. They're great kids and I love spending time with them while they're in our home. The chores often get done in an atmosphere of cooperation and happy banter. This feels ordinary yet extraordinary, a real blessing.

Our home feels peaceful and welcoming, with a loving and relaxed atmosphere. It has become a place that is thoroughly enjoyed by my family, our dogs, and the many teenagers and adult friends who visit. It's a tremendous breakthrough for me to realize that my home has become the home my children's friends want to visit and stay at. Now, finally, the experience of cleaning is a healthy self-expression of inner peace and love for my family, our cherished belongings, and myself.

Here are some ideas that relate to the cleanliness of your home:

- Begin to notice if you find yourself either obsessively cleaning or not cleaning at all and living amid a very dirty or chaotic physical space. This might be a sign that you are dealing with a deeper issue that relates to cleaning.

- If you suspect that your relationship with cleaning is not healthy, think about why this might be. Some of you may immediately identify experiences that shaped this pattern in your adult life. Others of you may have no clue and may not care to go there. Still others may have an inkling why this is happening and may be ready to look at a deeper issue. Trust that working toward healing will move your life toward freedom and your true desires.

- Consider whether you might benefit from working with a professional to distinguish the original experiences—not to relive these, but to see them in the light of your now-adult self, to come to terms with the impact, and to begin healing.

- If you are blessed with a reasonable relationship to cleaning, keep it going. I applaud you and invite you to clean with products and supplies that you love.

- If it would benefit your life to hire housecleaning help and you can afford this, start looking for people to interview and get some quotes. There are fantastic people who love cleaning homes. You will know you've found one because he or she will sparkle with joy when talking about cleaning homes. You may also find someone who is low-key and very competent. Ask friends for referrals.

- If you have children living at home, keep in mind that they learn what they live. Consider creating an atmosphere in which cleaning up is a joy. The results of having some moments of breathing room, tranquility, and clarity are well worth the effort. A tidy home (as it fits your standards) can be immensely gratifying.

- Be gentle with any process of healing you may choose in developing a healthier relationship with cleaning. There will be setbacks and slipups, and that's okay. Each moment is a new moment to grow and change and evolve. You might take two steps forward and then five steps backward; steps backward are part of the process. Take two steps forward again. And again. And again. You can do it.

- Look through your cleaning supplies, take inventory, and consider throwing away any items that are really old or ones you don't like to use. Cull through the rag bag. Consider using cleaning supplies that support the well-being of you and your family. Release or repair the broken vacuum cleaner.

- Schedule a party or small gathering as an inspiration for cleaning. Sometimes cleaning for others leads you to recognize that having a clean home can be a way to love others and yourself. Cleaning the spaces and belongings we love can be a way to show reverence and gratitude.

- Consider combining cleaning with clearing away unwanted belongings. Take it one room at a time and be gentle with yourself or work at a pace that satisfies your spirit. Deep cleaning and clearing take time and are well worth the breathing room and freedom.

## THE ORANGE TOOTSIE POP
*Living with the Love and Loss of a Pet*

Sitting at the table laughing and bantering while playing a game of Cranium, my family and I abruptly stop when we hear the noises of a very sick dog. She showed no signs of illness during the day, but I realize the cancer may have returned. It's a week and a half before Thanksgiving and we've had almost a year since her surgery. I feel my feet go out from under me, a sensation that would remain the next several days.

After all the presents had been opened on Christmas morning six years earlier, my husband had surprised our children with a treasure hunt, complete with interesting clues. They had squealed, brainstormed, shouted out possible locations, and rushed to the next area of our home looking for these messages. They still tease my husband for hiding the gift-wrapped dog gear in the dryer, of all places. We had captured on video the shrieks of joy when they saw the dog gear and reacted as though an actual dog had jumped out of the dryer. The room had exploded with their enthusiasm and joy!

All four of us met her at a farm three days later. From the moment she and I saw one another, we connected and I felt an instant rush of love. It was as though she had been waiting for me her whole life, like she knew me, everything about me, and *still* loved me. As a child I had wished fervently for a dog, knowing full well that it could never be—not in that home. A dog could never have survived there; I barely did. In the moment when I met her, a childhood dream came true for me as an adult.

She was an older dog of seven years with the given name "Weasel." This reminded me of smarmy guys from high school, so I said that I couldn't have a dog with this name. My husband mentioned that we could give her a new name, but for it to stick, it would have to sound a lot like her given name. I love *The Sound of Music*, so in an inspired moment I realized we could call her Liesel, after the oldest daughter of the Von Trapp family. Liesel's personality wasn't even remotely like this coming-of-age character; the connection begins and ends with the name.

Being a standard wire-haired dachshund, Liesel stubbornly barks and wags her tail simultaneously at everyone who comes to our door. She loves walking and sniffing the perimeter of our backyard when she's outside. I never figured out why she obsessively licks her paws like some people chain smoke. We have found partially chewed-up paper, paperback books, and even hardcover books on the floor, and we've slowly learned to keep things up and out of her sight. Our family vigilance finally aligned when a school project of our son's got eaten except for a tiny corner piece.

A year before my joyous meeting of Liesel, I had firmly and with clarity ceased all contact with my family of origin, all of whom blindly slogged around inside various destructive patterns. Since joining our family, Liesel has seen me through the most intense chapters of my ongoing recovery and healing from an abusive past that had extended into adulthood. I felt vividly the spiritual message she brought me—"You are deeply loved, Laura"—as I engaged some of the hardest work of my life. With everything she was and everything she did, she was this message. Even my husband can turn on me and I can turn on him; we clean it up and restore our kinder ways with each other, but then the cycle repeats. But Liesel never, ever turns on me, and I never, ever turn on her. She brings her lovable self to me, and I notice I bring my best self to her.

No matter what, she's happy to see me, tracking me everywhere I go in our home. As soon as I sit down in any room, she jumps up to sit with me. In the past year, when she couldn't jump anymore, she has put her front paws up on the chair, tongue lolling, and looked at me with her brown eyes hopeful for a lift up onto the seat with me, which I've always obliged.

For more than a year, I have medicated her eyes 10 times a day. With each dose I have let her know I care. Always compliant with this ritual, she has allowed me to love her in this unique way. I recognize I am capable of this depth, quality, and uncomplaining consistent care of a beloved other. It feels seamless and easy with my Liesel girl. The vet tells me all she can probably see is shadows, shapes, and movement. She always knows who I am, even when she loses this ability with my daughter, husband, and son. She barks at them and stops only when she recognizes their smells. She never barks at me. She knows me with every sense and hair on her cute low-rider body.

A few months after those visits to the veterinary eye doctors, Liesel had two different tumors removed, and she and I teamed up in a post-surgical healing dance. It involved me carrying her 29-pound body around carefully and constantly for about two weeks. After her sutures were removed, we chose to take no further action and place our intentions on creating the best quality of life we could for her.

Autumn arrived. I celebrated a birthday, and my friends commented on how quiet and well-behaved my Liesel girl was on this special day. Knowing food could fall at any moment, she watched and waited. Like so many dogs, she loves food. She licked the cake topper that accidentally fell on the floor. It was rescued in time for people to sing "Happy Birthday" as I held the Liesel-kissed topper above my vanilla cupcake.

Her message of unconditional love washes over me as we put away the board game and I clean up the mess she has made on the carpet. Starting on this night, when we realize how ill she is, she starts declining rapidly and yet her love for me grows and breathes inside all of me. Her love is impossible for me to ever forget, even in the moments when I am all alone, as it seems that I am when I walk inside the vet's office a week later for the procedure that will end Liesel's painful suffering and her amazing life.

When I return home, our house seems too quiet, too lonely even with our other dog, Lynzee, still very much alive. The rest of the day, I find all kinds of reasons to be out of the house, usually taking Lynzee with me. I find myself craving an orange Tootsie Pop, the childhood candy I loved. I have no idea why this grips me, distracts me; I rarely eat candy, let alone crave it! It's the second full day of grieving and I'm on a mission. On this unusually warm day in November, I bike to a BP station in search of a Tootsie Pop. They have every other candy there: Payday, Kit Kat, Skittles, and so many other colorful packages giggling back at me. I keep scanning each row for the Tootsie Pop. None. I buy two Peppermint Patties and eat both of them. No satisfaction.

After dinner that night, the kids are hungry for Oreos—an excuse to be out of the house! In my grief-driven state, I drive first to a natural foods grocery store to pick up some items for our Thanksgiving dinner. I then drive all the way to a mainstream grocery store in an entirely different section of town. I'm in my body, but not in my body as I walk into that brightly lit store knowing there must be Tootsie Pops in *this* store. I don't want a whole bag, though—just one orange Tootsie Pop!

I find the candy aisle and keep pacing up and down in search of a reasonably sized bag of Tootsie Pops. I feel kind of crazy because it is kind of crazy. They have big bags of Tootsie Pops filled with lots of brown and purple ones … gross. I walk down another aisle and return several times to the candy aisle in vain. Finally, I purchase the Oreos and make my way home. I have no idea how long I've been gone, but on the way, my husband calls.

"Where are you?" he asks.

"On my way …" I can tell I'm resisting going home even though people and another dog are there.

I tell my husband he could make my Thanksgiving by finding me an orange Tootsie Pop. I encourage him emphatically not to buy the whole bag. On Thanksgiving morning, I walk downstairs to feed Lynzee. In her food bowl is one glorious orange-wrapped confection with a white stick. I cry, feeling happy, sad, grateful, and moved. Later, I ask him about the whole bag thing and he pleads the fifth. Then our son blurts out, "Hey, Dad! Where's the stash of Tootsie Pops, because I'd love one!" At this point, I'm laughing.

Christmas morning arrives. My children and husband put gifts around me, and one in particular is tagged from my husband. I open it to find a beautiful container, the perfect size for Liesel's cremains. I lift the lid and it is filled with orange Tootsie Pops. I cry. He doesn't even realize he purchased a dual-purpose container! He shares his story of the search and all the different gas stations he visited. I feel completely touched by this simple, meaningful, and heartfelt gift.

I know this candy will never even remotely bring back Liesel or the feeling of her near me. I can only go to my imagination, my memories. Deep love and gratitude hold my sadness. I share the remaining treats with my kids and those who come to visit. When the container eventually stands empty, it will await the arrival of the ashes of this precious being. She will live on as my forever Liesel girl, my friend, my dog, the being who taught me unconditional love.

Pets enhance the experience of love and deep connection in our lives. If you enjoy pets, I hope you will embrace them in your life in ways that are meaningful to you. Perhaps it would work better for you to volunteer working with pets rather than to have one.

As I learned, the flip side of bringing a pet into your life is that you may need to say goodbye to that pet because of the unfortunate differences in our life spans. When you are grieving the loss of a pet, trust yourself and tune into your needs. Some people have to put away photos and then, in time, get them out again. Some must keep many photos of their beloved pet visible, either indefinitely or during the time of intense grieving. Some people create pet memorials on a table or in a corner of a room. Some people release every item associated with a pet. Sharing with compassionate friends and family helps, too. For some grieving pet owners, adopting another pet becomes a focus and a joy; other people are not ready for that step. Gratitude and love are powerful balms in times of loss. Focusing on all the things we love about our cherished pet can help the process.

I encourage you to be gentle with yourself as you grieve, and know that whatever you choose is working if you can keep staying connected to here and now. If you are neglecting yourself, others, work, hobbies, or other important aspects of your life, please seek out the help of a professional or support group.

Whether or not we have pets, we can learn many lessons

from their approach to life. For example, dogs teach us to be here now. Be friendly with most everyone you meet unless it's not an option. Walk. Run. Swim. Jump. Chase and catch your dreams. Bring them back for loved ones to enjoy. Eat with gusto. Be loyal to those who care. Sleep soundly. Love.

Cats teach us, for example, to be real at any moment. Shift who you are as necessary—playful, resourceful, cuddly, persistent, lovable, hissy, aloof, independent, reliable, sweet, smart, silly, and laser-like focused. Pounce on things that interest you, and find a sunbeam to nap in. You will still be loved and accepted and fed.

## I-SPYING, MIND-MELDING, AND SEEKING
## HIDDEN TREASURES
*Identifying Your Organizational Style*

O ver the years, I have discovered several ways that I—and most people I know—seem to organize belongings. Some ways have come as reactions to my childhood home. My dad, a paper accumulator, had difficulty letting go of pieces of paper. My mom was much like the hoarders shown in current TV shows. She kept almost everything, and our basement quickly became a holding container for all kinds of unwanted, unloved, and unused belongings. The attic became a storage area of nostalgia. She kept every meaningful outfit she ever wore and every fancy dress my sister and I ever wore, including bridal gowns, prom dresses, and bridesmaid dresses. My mom kept a fairly organized and well-functioning kitchen (complete with junk drawers, of course), but in storage areas, she stashed things and held on to these belongings for dear life.

I kept my side of my shared bedroom extremely neat and tidy, in a desperate attempt to create calming order in the midst of volatile people, especially my mother and sister. I also had the unfortunate experience of having beloved belongings randomly thrown in the trash as punishment. I still don't know what I did wrong, and maybe there's no real answer. A raging adult, towering over me, took treasures from my hands, and the threat of physical violence often met with the reality.

I learned quickly to not want things, or rather to hide my desire for things I truly loved. I also learned that I had to accept the tastes and preferences of my sister and my mom and appear grateful for things that they insisted on giving me. I felt invisible. I grew up suppressing most of my unique tastes or looking for small places where their tastes and mine intersected. To organize the few belongings I actually liked, I usually hid them under my bed, where they were safe and out of sight. I noticed that if belongings stayed under my bed, no one actually took them from me. Creating physical order in my spaces became a strategy to find a sense of safety and clarity.

Now with older children, I find my organizational styles shaped by these early experiences. I still crave order and tidiness, and I throw papers away regularly. I live at the other end of the spectrum from my dad with paper clutter, though occasionally a pile or two might get stacked. I keep this stack fairly visible and immediate; it reminds me of the day's priorities.

I'm the mom who knows where everything is and often finds things that were lost. I call this organizational style *Mind-Melding*: the ability to both store things in an organized way and remember where things are stored. "Mom, where's the can opener?" "Mom, where's my OSU buckeye necklace?" "Where are the glue sticks and poster board?" I can answer all of these immediately. These and other items are stored out of sight to keep flat surfaces free for their intended purpose.

People who enjoy this organizational style intuitively know where things are, even behind closed doors and cabinets. They can tell you from afar exactly where the keys, chargers, and candy stash are. They rarely rifle through cabinets and drawers in search of phones, rubber bands, or pens; they just know and remember! Extreme stress may throw off a Mind-Melder's gift, but usually this is temporary.

Mind-Melders feel best when they can walk into a relatively pristine space. Mind-Melders open file cabinets to pull out their

current work in progress and return that project to its spot at
the end of each day. Mind-Melding makes it easy to keep the
environment looking calm and uncluttered. People highly sen-
sitive to other people's detritus are probably this type. To people
with different organizational styles, the spaces organized by
Mind-Melders feel barren, too clean, and maybe unnerving.

Some people, like my father, feel soothed by having everything in the open where it can be seen. This is an organizational
style I refer to as *I-Spying*. I have this style in only certain rooms
and places. In my kitchen, I like having the toaster on the
counter to make toast for my family each morning. I enjoy
seeing the basket of bread, the bowl of apples, and the books on
my shelves. I love my blue teapot that sits on top of my stove.
As with the "I Spy" game, these things are within my field of
vision, and I (and others) can get them easily for use.

I-Spyers use their eyes as the source point. They are visually
cued, and they need to be able to walk into a room with a view
of some part of their work in progress. If things are put away,
they feel adrift and incapable of locating things. They are the
paper stackers on top of desks, and their projects lounge on
shelves. Open baskets with brightly colored yarns, beads, and
crafts entice them to create. They do not clear a desk at the end
of the day; instead, they place items in plain sight. They see
and embrace active chaos. To I-Spyers, a room with visual cues
looks beautiful, cheerful, and inspiring. Productivity and joyful
creativity happens easily.

Conversely, a room where everything is put away can be
stressful or disorienting for an I-Spyer. Worse, it can cause the
I-Spyer to forget about possessions and projects in progress.
Out of sight is indeed out of mind for people with this sort
of organizational style, who will entirely lose sight of projects

being worked on or books they were reading because their "bookmarks" are now hidden.

The third organizational style, *Hidden Treasure Seeking*, is the one I practiced in my childhood. With this style, the person occasionally stashes things in odd places to discover them later, often with joy and sometimes with shock that the item was even saved. Hidden Treasure Seeking seems to be something many people do. They stash stuff in such places as their purse, a drawer in the kitchen, a basket on top of the counter, the coat closet, or the glove compartment. Hidden Treasure Seekers often know where they've put things, but not always; they do eventually find what they need.

The drive to find what was stashed motivates Hidden Treasure Seekers to engage in seek-and-rescue missions. They make time to find what was once tucked away. The drawer gets opened and sorted through, the basket gets emptied, and the important items are found.

For most Hidden Treasure Seekers, finding hidden treasures can remind us of something about our humanity, our strengths, and our forgotten talents. Belongings we hide away may hold a truth about who we have been, which also gives us insight about who we really are and who we can become. The courage to go through (and cull, when needed) our belongings becomes well worth the effort and sometimes a necessity in our ever-changing lives.

Mind-Melding, I-Spying, and Hidden Treasure Seeking in our homes and lives are some ways to organize belongings and can be seen as metaphors for the different ways we've found to create meaning, calm, and clarity. At their extremes, they may not create optimal living environments. Take a moment and identify your style. How is it working for your life now?

Our homes teach us about ourselves; they often are the outer expression of our inner world, of our deepest fears and desires. We get to choose what we want to learn from our homes. Your organizational style reveals something about how you create, produce, and enjoy your life inside your home.

Here are some ideas to consider regarding the organizational styles we use in our homes:

- Identify the preferred organizational style of everyone in your home. This makes it easier to honor each person's style and help him or her organize belongings in ways that feel calming and safe. Some people (the Mind-Melders) may feel best with everything inside cabinets, closets, and drawers. Others (the I-Spyers) may thoroughly enjoy seeing their mementos and unfinished projects in full view. And finally, the Hidden Treasure Seekers like to play hide-and-seek with their belongings. You can embrace the game even if this isn't your style.

- Remember that a certain degree of organization supports mental clarity. If you are struggling with confusion, consider looking at your physical space for pockets of disorganization that don't feel right to you, and take action to organize them. Seek the support of organized friends or a professional organizer, if needed.

- Think about your belongings as a story about you and your life. If you have unresolved trauma, grief, or loss in your life experience, this part of your story may also exist somewhere in your home as a metaphor, an outside picture of that challenging time. Consider working gently to bring completion with the belongings you associate with that painful experience. Letting go of belongings that have powerful associations but are no longer loved and used can be some of the bravest feng shui work you can do. In other situations, you might find it healing to find different places for those belongings, moving them from hidden spaces to visible ones or vice-versa.

- Consider the junk room or junk drawer in your home as an opportunity to create a shift in your life experience. Finding (and processing) the treasures in these spaces could be incredibly fruitful, especially if you are living through a life transition and need time to sort through and process the emotions associated with those belongings. Taking them out is an opportunity to envision the space for a future that awaits you and to take small actions each day to create a space you love and the opportunities you would love to flow into your life. Letting go of unloved, unused belongings and organizing the ones that you do love and use often allows for uplifting experiences.

## THERE'S NO PLACE LIKE HOME
*Finding What Can Never Be Lost*

After a warm, beautiful spring day, the wind blows strong and the air, now biting cold, stings. A gate remains open when it should have been closed. A four-legged member of the family, undaunted by the chill, seizes the opportunity.

Upstairs, I flip the covers off the bed, preparing to go to sleep, and I hear yelling. My husband discovers the backyard gate was left open. "Layla got out! The gate was open!" The bellowing, fear-driven, angry voice of my usually unflappable man fills the whole house.

*Really?* I think to myself as this incredible calm washes over me, or maybe it's dissociation or a bone-deep exhaustion, as I crawl into bed longing for sleep and warmth. *Layla, come home* clear as a bell speaks from deep inside me. The image of her dachshund face, her brown eyes staring at me, downloads in my mind's eye. My husband leaves the house and returns moments later. I call from the bed, "Did you find her?"

"No, I'm leaving in my car to look for her!" Our son gets on his bike to search as well.

Again, I experience a perfect calm, a confidence and clarity that she is safe. I know she'll come home. But I still climb out of bed; I pull on sweats, socks, and a coat and walk to our front porch. I walk out the side door to the back yard. Someone must have closed the gate. I open it, knowing she needs access for her return. "Layla!" I call out in a clear, firm voice with no trace of fear. "Layla!" I'm suddenly keenly aware that we have neighbors and it's 10:30 p.m. on a Sunday night. I return to the front porch as the cold air and lights envelop me. I see no movement. All remains still and quiet everywhere I move and look.

My daughter joins the remote search party, and I promise to call from home base with any news. After awhile, I call them all: "Come home. She's a smart girl. She knows where we live and that we love her." These words flow out of me from a place of deep knowing that feels very unfamiliar to me. My words rarely flow from such clarity and confidence. Mostly they originate from a jabbering, blathering, anxious, neurotic place of freaking out about both little and big and meaningless and meaningful stuff I can't control.

My son returns, angry and scared. He's upset with himself and admits he probably left the gate open, but like many people, he blames his mom. "Why didn't you put her collar on? Why didn't you check all the gates before you let her out? We need to put a GPS on her collar!" I listen intently and feel both his fear and anger. I say nothing. He loves the dogs; he's loved all the dogs that have been a part of our family, bonding quickly and deeply with each one. He feels a special bond with Layla because she embodies an adventurous and fierce protective spirit that matches his own. He too has taken a couple nighttime teenage adventures. I realize that Layla's breakout is allowing him to experience what it feels like to love and care for someone and have her disappear, to not know where she is or if she is safe.

When my daughter and husband return, I remain certain. "I encourage all of you to shift from fear and anger to imagining her with you, being with her, feeling relief and love for her. She'll come home." I assure my kids we'll let them know when Layla returns, and they reluctantly slink off to bed. My daughter joins me in this place of clarity when I hug her goodnight. "She'll come home, Mom." Less confident, my husband camps out in the living room on the blow-up mattress, with lights illuminating the foyer and the porch. The glass storm door serves as a window for us and for our wanderer.

Back in bed more images enter my mind's eye in full color. I see a scene from *Because of Winn-Dixie* when the dog returns after the thunderstorm and I hear the song they sing in celebration; I see red slippers on Layla's paws clicking together and Judy Garland declaring "There's no place like home." Lastly, I envision a quick flash of her still body and her whole wiggly self. Again, booming with power, the words *Layla come home!* vibrate inside me.

This phrase repeats more gently and peacefully, soothing me to sleep. A clear picture of her face accompanies the words. I wake up with a start at 1:30 a.m. Immediately, I think *Layla, come home.* It consumes me; I become the mantra. I hear my husband crinkle off the plastic mattress, open the front door, and whistle softly. He returns to the mattress and to snoring. What seems like a moment later, I hear it: "Arf!" I bound out of bed, rush down the stairs, and see her in the flood of lights. *She's here!* Standing on our welcome mat, Layla looks up at me through the clear storm door. I open the door and crouch down with arms open wide. It's a blissful, joyful, face-licking, body-wiggling, bouncy reunion. She's here!

My husband stands next to us. Layla greets him and then moves to her water bowl for a long drink. "Yeah, that dead squirrel sure tastes salty," my husband says. It's his way of saying, "I'm so glad you're home, but you scared the crap out of me, you stupid, lovable dog!" He shares with me that he dreamt that she came to the front door and then he awoke to my footsteps on the stairs.

I scoop her up to take her to my son's bedroom. He sits up in his bed and I hand him our Layla. I feel his relief, his love. I say nothing. No apology or forgiveness is required. Love fills his room.

We'll never know where Layla went on her three-and-a-half-hour nighttime adventure, but it sure solidifies an experience of deeper truths, magic, mystery, the power of calm confidence, and the wisdom of staying grounded in the midst of life's curveballs. Maybe there's something to the sound and majesty of silence and what emerges from that sacred and quiet place. Maybe stillness and quiet is where home really is.

Sometimes life roars with chaos around us. We can be like the monk climbing the mountain holding a bowl of water during a thunderstorm without sloshing a drop, but then the monk didn't have two kids, two dogs, and a husband. Maybe finding stillness takes some practice, but it's well worth the effort. It may be where we find sanity, deeper wisdom, and an ability to respond with equanimity to life's unexpected adventures.

Here are some ideas to consider for cultivating calm in the midst of life's curve balls:

- Depending on what works for you, try meditation or time to be still and quiet, or dance to a song that makes you get up and dance! (How about "Le Freak" by Chic or "Staying Alive" by the Bee Gees?)
- Set a goal like taking a yoga class, training for a half marathon, or focusing your senses on five things to see, touch, taste, smell, or feel, to help you focus on something other than the chatter in your mind.

- Set aside time to steep yourself in whatever setting relaxes you and makes you feel most alive. For some people, it might be a bustling urban environment, and for others, it might be a natural setting with trees, flowers, grass, flowing water, and rocks.

- Read or listen to your favorite source of spiritual comfort.

- Take a break from the news or unplug from social media for a specific time period, whether it's a month or an hour. You might find yourself looking at a tree or a loved one as if for the first time.

- Choose to clear your diet of food and beverages your body can't stand. Listen to your body; it will tell you what these might be. Or if you normally take this approach, you can occasionally indulge in a treat you otherwise would not. I love the gluten-free cupcakes where they take out the gluten and put in extra sugar.

- Ignore all the above and go about living your life. No worries.

## MY HAWAIIAN TILE
*Creating a Kind "Hello" at the Entrance to Your Home*

Walking over the huge slab of concrete, some of which is breaking down into smaller chunks and tiny pieces, my husband and I leave for a walk on a late summer morning. I put voice to a wistful thought. "It would be so great to have our porch tiled before family members come for my birthday in October. I wish we had purchased that tile we loved, and stored it until you could work on it."

Months ago, the "tile the front porch" project had vacated the "back burner"—and the stovetop completely—for a variety of reasons. Until I walked gingerly over the broken concrete today, I had made peace with this, knowing that the transformation of our home would happen over time.

As we walk through our favorite neighborhood park in the streaming sunshine, my husband agrees that we could have made that purchase when we found the tile pattern we both loved. He also notes that we didn't. He says nothing more. Feeling the discomfort of this exchange, I quickly change the subject to the kids and the logistics of the day.

A few weeks later on our morning walk, my husband touches my arm, looks at me, and asks, "Would you really love to have the porch tiled for your birthday?"

I enthusiastically reply, "Yes, that would be great! I'd love it!"

He continues, "Well, a long time ago I set aside some money. It was for something else, but I could use it for this."

I'm genuinely surprised. "Really? But wait, what did you have the money set aside for?" I'm so curious and I want to know.

He hesitates. "It's not important."

Now I'm really curious. I persist, "What? Was it a motor-cycle? I know you've wanted one ever since your mom said over her dead body, but she's very much alive at 88. You've got to tell me. I really want to know!" He shrugs his shoulders in silence.

A fear thought wisps across my mind: *Oh my God, he has a love child, and he has the stash for when this surprise offspring of the 1960s shows up!* Thank goodness my internal editor shows up for this conversation, because my mouth stays closed. Too many times in my life, she has left for lunch or a chai latte and freed my mouth to blab unfiltered comments right out into the world. I know all too well the hot, red-faced shame of her absence. Fortunately, I avert this completely.

Gently, I ask again. "What was the original intention for this money, Sweetheart?"

Finally, I see his whole body cave. He looks at me. "A long time ago, as a way to celebrate your birthday, I began a fund to take us on a trip to Hawaii, but logistics would be tough—what to do with the kids and the dogs? I don't know how it could have happened anyway."

Tears flood my eyes. He's not really the thoughtful type in this way. I say, "Really? That is *so* sweet!" I look at this man I've known for many years. He looks different to me, almost like I'm seeing him fresh and unguarded, like an altered, blurred image. It's not that I've never seen his romantic self, but this part of him seems to hide out with my oft-absent internal editor. I think they go on long European vacations together.

My children, appalled by my role reversal, insist that my husband and I go to Hawaii. My daughter says, "This is the dork who handed you a piece of paper with a check-the-box marriage proposal during halftime of an Ohio State game. *Mom*, he saved up to take you to Hawaii for your birthday!"

My son declares, "Mom, you've got to go to Hawaii!" For several days my daughter rolls her eyes when she looks at me. How could I choose tile over a Hawaiian vacation? The fact is that I do choose the tile. I choose it with conviction, clarity, and joy.

My husband works many hours cutting pieces, slathering them with soft gray goo, and laying them in as straight a pattern as the concrete slab will allow. The weather turns, bringing cold and rain. Ideally, the grout would have five dry days in a row to set properly. We cover the project with plastic held down by brooms and heavy ceramic pots. Nevertheless, time runs out and weather conditions sabotage the completion of the project.

Loving friends and family enter our home on my big day, my first adult birthday party. Like a red carpet laid over a muddy walkway, the beautiful tile leads people to the front door, although the edges of the porch remain unadorned with the new tile. Even in its incomplete state, the tile serves its greater purpose of providing a beautiful welcome.

This entrance upgrade ushers in so much joy in its first couple months. My sister-in-law stays a whole week after my party, and then my husband gets an unexpected call after Thanksgiving. Our beloved nephew, who serves in the Air Force and completed a tour of duty in Afghanistan, will be visiting us before the holidays. We haven't seen him in two years, and he hasn't been to our home in seven years. To me, these adored visitors seem less like a coincidence, and more like the result of clear intention and the welcoming feel of the tile ushering in good experiences and people.

My husband's birthday gift of labor and love creates a beautiful enhancement for the entrance to our home. Friends and neighbors comment on its beauty. I smile every time I leave the house through the front door to walk the dogs or to go for a run. The kids and I find ourselves in the spring spending time on the porch, enjoying the look and feel, especially after my husband places the last few pieces on the edges. As a "greeter" for friends, family, and neighbors and a constant "Welcome home" to us, the "Hawaiian" tile becomes a gift that keeps giving.

Here are ideas to consider when you enhance the entrance to your home:

- Experience the entrance to your home as if for the first time. Look for anything that blocks the pathway to the front door, and make a plan to remove these obstacles.

- Think about any warning signs you have posted out front. Such signs send a mixed message to friends and family who want to be with you and enjoy your company. Consider taking these signs down and trusting that your property is protected, especially if you've purchased a home alarm system. A peephole in your door may be a helpful addition to compensate for the removal of the sign, because you can check for unwanted strangers and salespeople.

- Ask yourself whether you can see the front door from the street. Are shrubs or trees blocking the view? Consider trimming down or removing and relocating large shrubs or trees, and planting low-to-the-ground flowers you love to open the view of the front door.

- Check whether the number of your house is visible from the street and there are lights at night for safety. It's optimal to design a safe passageway to your front door at any time of day or night.

- Remember that the front entranceway to your home symbolizes the gateway for people and life experiences to flow into your life. What beautiful and new opportunities do you anticipate streaming into your life? Are there some you'd like to create? Contemplate who might walk into your life and offer support, ideas, and inspiration for your life journey.

- Create entrances to your home that are safe and welcoming for you as well as all others.

- If you usually come in through the garage only, consider using your front door either occasionally or regularly. Also, make enhancements to the garage door entrance so it becomes an "I'm so happy to be home" space.

- If you use your back door as a primary door, create it to be safe and welcoming. At the same time, consider what's happening in your life, and look to see if there's an experience of "access denied" with regard to career, money, relationships, health, joy, or self-awareness. Start using your front door more often and making enhancements to that entrance, and see what happens.

- Think more broadly about entrances to and from your life. In times of transition, take advantage of the ripe opportunity to reflect on the support you would appreciate and the guidance you can give to others. Consider the flow of ideas exchanged, experiences that challenge you, and ones that embolden and carry you. Know you are never alone on your journey to the very next moment of your life. You are safe and welcome at many entranceways in life.

# A BELOVED BELONGING CHANGES HANDS
*Letting Go of Childhood Things*

For months I see it through the window as I stand at the stove cooking. Lonely and ignored by our two teenagers, it sits there, gathering leaves and spider webs, a reminder of more carefree and playful days. This structure holds rich memories from what seems like a lifetime ago. I see the images and hear the sounds of my preschool-aged son and daughter asking to be pushed in the scooped yellow seats, singing Raffi's "Down by the Bay," while struggling to pump their legs. I remember pulling the hose to the top of the bright yellow slide and creating a wet, cool, and slippery ride on a hot summer day.

I know this large wooden play structure drains energy, takes up space in the yard, and looks and smells like clutter. Yet I sense that none of us is ready to let it go. My entire family is gripping tightly to this intersection of wood, metal, plastic, and canvas. Agitated "No" responses fly my way when I mention removing it from the yard. This play equipment holds a comforting and joyful connection to the past at a time when the future seems uncertain. The tension builds between the intuitive knowledge that it must go and the sentimental desire to keep it.

In late July, my husband informs me, "Checks have not come for many hours of work I did in April, May, and June. The billing process has changed hands, and the new folks seem to be all thumbs." The breaking point has arrived: I remind my family that the play structure sits in what feng shui defines as the prosperity corner of our backyard and our entire property. Having steeped in these ideas with me for years, my family gets it. With this awareness and inspiration, each of us moves into action. I make phone calls to several charities and discover one that may accept the structure, but they need a photo. Within five minutes, my technology-savvy daughter takes a snapshot of the play structure and clicks "Send." Clarity about a more prosperous future leaves sentiment in the dust.

The next day, Habitat for Humanity calls to say that we can donate the play structure to them, but the organization does not have the resources to take it apart or pick it up. I quickly learn that it is expensive to hire someone to haul it away. This motivates my husband, who locates places where he can rent tools and a truck. Within days of my sending off the original email, my whole family has become united and enthusiastic to let go of the play structure. We're also excited that this beloved play equipment will have a new life with small children. My children wonder if the children will enjoy the slide and if they will invent games and adventures in the sandbox and from the platform. They hope the children will love this play structure as much as they had. Giving creates a joy in my two teenagers that fills my heart and theirs. The once lonely play structure will have a wonderful new life.

My husband and son work as an efficient and inspired duo dismantling the clubhouse. Two days later they load it onto a rental truck and drive to the west side of town. It becomes a memorable and happy adventure for both of them. When they come home, my son excitedly shares, "While driving the truck, Dad yelled at this woman driver who was texting, 'Don't text and drive!' And she shouted back, 'Kiss my A#$!' And then we saw a 1959 turquoise and white Chevrolet Bel Air, and Dad told me that's the exact car you and Dad drove to your wedding, Mom, and guess what else? We got the truck for free! We paid for the gas, but there was no rental fee! The lady took so long processing the paperwork that her boss told us we didn't have to pay! We *were* standing in that store for a really long time, Mom!"

The next day, two rebate checks come in the mail, and I find a dime and a penny in a parking lot. The very next day, I find a one-dollar bill on a road in our neighborhood. Two weeks later, several large checks arrive in the mail at my husband's office. These are just the first indicators of the many events that shift our financial picture. A month later, my husband receives a large check for all the work he did.

Our backyard prosperity corner, now with squares and rectangles of grass seed, holds open space. A future filling up with hope pulls on our hearts a bit more than the memories of the past do. We plan a trip to our favorite hiking trail in southern Ohio with our two dogs. My family realizes that our tomorrows invite possibilities and new adventures, too.

Perhaps you, too, are contemplating letting go of once-beloved belongings that are no longer being used. Here are some ideas that will help give you clarity as you ponder letting go of these things:

- Ask yourself some basic questions: *What would my life feel like without this belonging? What would I do with my time if I weren't wondering or worrying about this unused item? Are there people who could benefit from having this belonging in their lives?*

- Consider charting a possible future for your life. What experiences would you like to have? What haven't you done that you've been yearning to do? Imagine the freedom, time, and energy to create this adventure. Hold a vision in your mind and feel the excitement and joy of this experience happening.

- Remember that confusion is a train stop away from clarity. Listen to your heart's true desire underneath the mind's barrage of doubts and excuses. Anticipate the breathing room in the physical space once you release the unused belonging. It will be free and so will you!

- When things clog our lives, we feel clogged. Take a moment to notice this experience and then realize you can take action to clear the obstacles. Trust that you have everything you need to take this action and it's a choice to just let go of things you don't need. Consider it is as easy as putting a grocery item back on the shelf that you really don't need or want.

- Contemplate the possibility that as clarity of purpose and meaning in your life emerges and you shift your focus to this greater purpose and passion, it will become easy to let go gracefully. When we are fearful, we cling to things and people. Love, grace, and clarity often allow us to detach and say goodbye.

- Remember that your time is precious and how you spend your time matters.

CITY SLICKER GOES CAMPING

*Experiencing Adventures and Appreciating Home*

Going camping after 20 years seems like an intriguing idea. I remember the air, the trees, the sound of tires on the gravel roads, the welcome breather from loud machines, the sweetness of nature's music, and the coziness of sleeping in a tent. Because of previous experience, I give myself full permission to take an air mattress. Being gluten-free among hungry teenage cross-country runners, I also know to pack my own food. I'm one of four adult chaperones on an adventure to a community that borders Lake Michigan, which I've never seen. My courage steps forward as I lean into my love and passion for nature and those delicious ads on the radio for "Pure Michigan."

After traveling through intermittent rain and a powerful thunderstorm, we finally arrive. The sultry heat of reality seeps into the soggy ground. The campgrounds are a quarter mile away from a major freeway roaring with trucks and cars day and night. This deafening noise almost drowns out the crickets, cicadas, and birds. The soft pulses of natural quiet breathe somewhere else. Soap dispensers, too, have vacated the premises. I feel relief that there are showers with hot water, flush toilets, and sinks with working handles and running water. The bugs, spiders, and mud create an unforgettable community shower experience. I'm acutely aware that we've entered their "house."

Determined to be a happy camper, I arise early every morning and take a long nature walk with my water pack strapped

onto my waist. I walk on dunes that rise up unlike anything
I've seen or experienced. The white, sandy beach and blue lake
water soothe me. Smooth, colorful rocks replace the seashells
normally found on an ocean beach. The sounds of nature float
gently in this area of the park. I wish my tent could be right here,
especially at night. In this place of beauty, I miss my husband the
most. He's home taking care of the dogs, his work, and a one-
item to-do list.

My son and daughter and their teammates run twice a day
on this training trip and enjoy the outdoors the rest of the time.
It's heartening to experience a group of teenagers all unplugged,
for the most part. Cell phones, like cigarettes for chain smokers
trying to quit, appear in their hands for what I still call "Kodak
moments." They call them selfies; it's the new normal.

The sultry, stormy weather of earlier in the week clears to
gorgeous blue skies, cooler breezes, and brilliant sunshine. Everyone welcomes the shift. Yet I feel the pull of home, solid walls,
the seemingly dull white noise of our nearby expressway, our
"designed for astronauts" mattress, and the arms of my husband
holding me close. I gather all the female athletes, who had ridden
in my van on the way here, for the return home. They seem as
giddy as I am about going home.

Our first stop is a roadside rest area with restrooms complete
with black dispensers that magically squirt pink soap dollops into
our cupped hands. All of us squeal with delight. Ah, the simple
joy of experiencing really clean hands! I call my husband from
the road: "We are about 30 minutes from Columbus. Could you
please go to Starbucks and purchase a venti chai latte with two
pumps? You have no idea how happy this will make me!"

Utterly relieved to be home, I cry and run to hug my
husband in our garage. When I walk into our home, I see, feel,

and smell it … a clean house! This delights me, as does the hot tea he hands me. The one-item to-do list spontaneously and generously spawned several meaningful actions that create a beautiful look and feel in our home. He has repaired and anchored the stairway railing in our foyer. The railing has also been freshly painted after 10 years of us living with the way we inherited it. All the wood floors gleam from a bath and refinishing. Every shelf in the basement has been cleared and organized. I keep squealing and hugging my husband. It's my personal version of an adult Christmas morning.

I see my husband through fresh eyes. It feels like a revelation of sorts. His kind deeds around our house seem to have come from a commitment to please me, to bring me joy. I thought I had married a procrastinator who woke up in the morning thinking, *How can I annoy my wife today?* I still occasionally wrestle with the thought that others design their lives around making me a target for their pain. In reality, they are probably as self-absorbed as I am pretending not to be.

As with this camping adventure and my welcome home, there often exists a continuum of experiences, including ones that are pleasant, joyful, uncomfortable, disgusting, and energizing. Sometimes people and experiences surprise us because we have been so busy focusing on the bothersome, searching desperately for shiny objects to distract us, or not paying attention at all. Maybe the surprises in life are designed to wake us up and allow us to choose to be *all in* on this life journey. They are an invitation to live the adventure of being alive, of being willing to remain awake, mindfully aware of the complexity, angst, and beauty in others and inside of us. This can especially be true of the people, places, and spaces we cherish the most.

Here are some resources and ideas to consider:

- When you have extra money to spend, consider using it to purchase a memorable experience. Brain and positive psychology research shows that an experience provides more long-lasting happiness than an object does.

- Ask yourself what experiences you would love to have, and start creating them. Take small actions every day to have them happen! Adventures often bring surprise, delight, and usually a funny story to tell when you return home.

- Choose a day to stay alert and mindfully aware of everyone and everything that is happening around you. I encourage you to listen deeply and look fully at all of it. You may discover treasures and pains that free you to create a life you truly want.

THE GUY AT THE GYM

*Making Sure Your Furniture Fully Supports You*

Knowing that I have a green light, I begin my day inspired. After breakfast and a cup of tea with cream, I head to the family room. Based on a mapping tool done in feng shui, this is the love and marriage area of our first floor. I begin moving furniture, and with the exception of the television, all of it gets rearranged. It's part of my plan to easily remove the old furniture when I bring in the new.

My husband has finally realized we might need a new couch, thanks to what I call "the guy at the gym." Let me explain. On many occasions, I have made suggestions to my husband like "You would *love* this [book, movie, class] …!" and he has looked at me blankly, mumbled, or walked away. Then one day, seemingly out of the blue, he has walked in, uncharacteristically gestured with his arms, and said excitedly, "I just met this guy at the gym, who told me about this great [thing I suggested], and I'm going to [buy it or do it]!" Then within 24 hours, my partner has taken inspired action. Perhaps your loved ones also have encountered "guys at the gym" who make great suggestions that they seem not to have heard before.

This time, my husband's "guy at the gym" showed up as a colleague and her husband, who graciously opened their home for a holiday party. We got to sit on their amazing leather sectional, complete with electric reclining chair components. My husband was in heaven! He joked that all of us who were lounging might be moving in. I took all of this to heart and made mental notes of his joy. He asked his colleague and her husband all kinds of questions about their fabulous couch, and they happily shared details.

Months before, I had mentioned to him that our family room couches felt lumpy and bumpy and looked, as my teenagers would say, "kind of ratchet" (translation: grungy, yucky, worn-out, unsightly, gross, seriously unattractive). He had declared, "They're fine," and that was that. I'd made a handful of attempts to show him what I meant. Mostly, he had just walked away to leave for work. Maybe part of the problem had been my timing. Transitions aren't a great time to propose ideas.

We returned from the holiday gathering. Standing together in our family room, he finally saw what my children and I had been seeing for months. He said, "Man, these couches are really old, Sweetheart. How long have we had them?"

I think to myself, *He's actually going to hear my answer. I can feel it.* "Seventeen years."

He was surprised. "Wow, really? We definitely need to get either a sectional or a new couch, preferably leather with the built-in recliner." In this moment, I wished I could bear-hug his colleague and her husband. Now aligned as a couple, we happily began the search for new furniture.

So thanks to his colleagues and their lovely sectional, I stand in the family room, perspiring from rearranging the furniture, and anticipate our trip to the furniture store the next day.

As we sit in our van looking in the windows of a large sofa store, my husband says, "Remember, these furniture salespeople can be high pressure. We are definitely *only looking*." Because I've spent so much of my life looking for love and other things in all the wrong places, I'm overjoyed to be walking into a furniture store looking for furniture! Having moved around the couches in my family room and considered some possibilities, I feel ready to find options that will work in our home.

Thankfully, the man who offers his help seems kind and genuinely helpful, not pushy or overbearing at all. I like him. I remind myself I'm not here to make friends, just look for a sectional or a couch and chair—leather, a color we both love, and comfortable to sit in. We find ones we like and have fun sitting on several sectionals and couches, even ones way out of our price range. It's part of the adventure. We get measurements and a business card from the salesman.

Standing in our family room later, we assess the measurements and realize a sectional won't work. Equipped with this knowledge, my husband takes additional action. The next day I get a phone call from him. "Hey, I'm at another furniture store and found this couch and chair, floor models, on clearance! They'll make us a great deal!" His enthusiasm flows through the phone. I have this thought: *He's going to buy this couch if I don't slow him down.* When he gets clear about something, mountains move!

I reply, "Okay. And we are still only looking, right?"

He says, "Yes, but I want you to see it. Let's come here on Friday!"

Before Friday he shows me a picture on the computer of this double-recliner couch. I see something altogether different than a couch. "Someone lied to you! That is two recliners shoved together for two really fat men! A couch has visually cued seating for three."

Taken aback, he says, "You could've just said you didn't like it."

I reply, "Okay. You're right. But there is only one seam down the middle. It's not a couch!"

Friday arrives and we pay a visit to this couch or whatever it actually is. The saleswoman invades my personal space. She asks, "Isn't it pretty?"

My old self, trained in pretending, would've quickly agreed, but that's no longer who I am. I stand silently for what feels like five minutes and then look at the saleswoman with a grimace and shake my head.

She backs off by saying, "I know. We find that most women think it looks like a recliner." I could never be this kind of salesperson. The couch was awful and ugly. Its color, mushroom, works better sautéed with onions in a skillet. My husband and I sit down on it. He isn't a large man, but he isn't small, either. Both of us fit on one whole side of this double-wide. We stand up and quickly make our motions to leave. The saleslady is lurking so closely that she bumps into us, business card in hand. We thank her politely and almost run to the escalator. We laugh heartily when we get to the van.

Within two weeks we find a couch and chair we love with the reclining components. They fit perfectly in our family room. As a family, we enjoy watching favorite TV programs and movies on Sunday evenings. It has been an adventure and one that was worth the wait, so I'm grateful for "the guy at the gym." However, I think that next time I have a cool idea, I'm going to take it viral with all my husband's friends, colleagues, neighbors, and "gym-mates."

Here are some ideas to consider when buying furniture:

- Research using the internet during the early stages of buying furniture, if you'd like. Once you've narrowed down your options, though, it's important to touch, smell, sit in, and stand close to any furniture you are committed to having in your home or office. Colors on a computer screen look different in person, and you can know the comfort level of a couch only by sitting on it.

- Measure furniture and the space it is intended for, and make sure these numbers align. This seems obvious, but sometimes we forget about these details. Measure first, and then allow yourself to fall head over heels in love with it.

- Shop for furniture as though you are dating to make sure you find just the right one. Listen to the wise matchmakers who stay a safe distance away, ask details about your ideal type, listen to your list of qualities, honestly guide you toward the field of possible matches, and trust you to pick the one you love!

- Experience furniture for its comfort and safety. Avoid purchasing any type of furniture that could harm you or the ones you love. This includes sharp-cornered tables, really uncomfortable chairs, and furniture with parts that are close to the floor and can easily stab your toes. Remember that some furniture design is really beautiful but is best experienced by your eyes and brain only.

- Consider the size of any furniture you are buying and your size as well. Tall cabinets and shelving units are perfect for tall people. If you're short and love (or already have) high shelves, get yourself a sturdy stepstool and plan on using it a lot. If you need a ladder to get into your bed or have to do the run-and-jump, your bed may not be quite the right size for you and may not give you the sense of safety you need in order to feel rested.

- Carry out of your home today any piece of furniture that you loathe or that makes you feel agitated, annoyed, paranoid, or fearful, or choose the date when it will be gone. If this is impractical (perhaps because others in the home like the furniture as much as you dislike it), look for ways to soften or balance this item. Consider placing a beloved blanket on the couch you can't stand or favorite books on the shelving unit that does not reflect your tastes. Keep moving in the direction of living with furniture you love.

- Work within if it is not the right time to make a purchase. When we truly cannot alter our physical surroundings, we sometimes need to work within ourselves to live with love. Look for ways to find internal peace, comfort, and safety inside yourself, in your imagination, and outside your home. Often the outer physical changes are the last to shift; the work can start on the inside and move outward.

# A PASSAGEWAY FOR JOY
*Designating a Space for Creative Expression*

My son turned six just after we moved into what he nicknamed "the rusty house." It took me a moment to understand this phrase, but then I noticed that along with really old carpeting and many signs of neglect, all the windows in this grand old home had rust flaking in the metal lines of the casement crank-outs. The "eyes" of this house, crusted over inside their lids, barely opened to let in fresh air, sunlight, and the breezes of springtime. Replacing all these windows became a high-priority item on a very long list.

Although I knew it needed attention, the long upstairs hallway barely made the list of home repairs. Scraping off the wallpaper in this hallway and elsewhere throughout the house became my mission. I eventually ventured into the long hallway and peeled away the old skin of its walls. For weeks, I juggled this deep transformation project with the care of my children, who were becoming bored as the rain kept them from venturing into the backyard. They drew on paper with crayons and played with small toys on the floor of the living room, an area that felt safe to them, but they were yearning for a different outlet. An idea bubbled up inside of me.

"Let's go buy some paints for both of you … all different colors!"

They looked at me with such joy on their faces. "Okay, Mommy!"

Once we were back from the store, I set them up in the

long hallway, now relieved of its yellowed wallpaper. I grabbed a stepstool and let both children know they could paint everywhere on these walls in the hallway. My son, overjoyed, climbed the stepstool and began painting with sweeping strokes. "Look, Mommy, I'm an artist!" My seven-year-old daughter stood at another wall and painted two houses complete with walkways.

That autumn, we noticed so many leaves changing. We walked outside and gathered different ones: maple, oak, and others I couldn't identify in hues of yellow, red, greenish yellowish, and brown. My daughter became so excited. "Let's make leaf rubbings, Mom! We've been doing them in art class. It's so much fun!" We gathered supplies and placed them on the dining room table. I watched crayons gently moving back and forth on white paper, magically creating another colorful, waxy leaf imprint.

"Mommy, I could paint a tree on the wall upstairs and we could put these leaves on that tree," my daughter said, running to find the brown paint and brushes. They painted the tree and its branches, and then filled them with the cut-out, taped-on leaves we'd rubbed.

The next Halloween, my son wanted to be a leaf bag. At first I resisted, knowing that I couldn't glue actual leaves to his bag. However, I remembered the leaves stuck to the tree on the wall. We walked upstairs and gently peeled them off the tree, which now had a wintertime look. With the crayon leaves securely taped onto the bag and holes cut out for his head and arms, his costume was complete. He won a "most creative" prize at a neighborhood Halloween parade.

A year later, before Thanksgiving, my son surprised me with a turkey on the wall, which joined the leafless tree and other drawings. "I did it all by myself, Mommy!" My daughter had

named the turkey John. From swooshes of color on the wall to
a tree with (and then without) leaves to a turkey with a name,
these walls had been a place of creativity for my children. I kept
thinking that in a few years, I would paint the hallway and hang
real artwork or family photos.

Instead, the brown painted tree stayed in a dormant, leafless state as our lives moved forward through many seasons.
New creative life for the wall emerged when my daughter began
high school. Her new friends, intrigued by the unfinished
hallway walls of art, asked if they could draw on them. I said
yes. Words of love, quotes from movies, doodles, tic-tac-toe
games, and friends' signatures filled the empty spaces on the
hallway walls.

When we discussed painting the wall, all of us felt some
sadness mixed with a sense of closure. It was time for change.
Some of my daughter's closest friends made certain to take one
last look and remember. As we approached my daughter's graduation from high school and her graduation party at our home,
my husband finally painted the walls of this hallway a lovely
soft shade of blue.

We had attended several graduation parties and I had noticed
a theme of photo memories displayed in different ways at each of
these celebrations. A month before my daughter's party, I had an
idea. On one of the hallway walls, I displayed photos of her with
friends and family from birth forward. I included song lyrics,
quotes, and sayings as a gift of love and a celebration of her life so
far. The experience uplifted me even as I grieved her childhood
coming to an end. The hallway wall fulfilled the need for one last
creative burst.

As I take down the photos and phrases, I feel grateful and
nostalgic for this wall and how it held space for my children's

creations and joyful expressions, and those of their friends; how it changed over time and invited me to share my love for my daughter. In some ways, this long hallway became one of my favorite places to walk slowly through and savor in the midst of movement, growth, and change.

Here are some ideas to nurture creative expression in your home:

- If you have children, look for an area of your home where they can feel free to create. It may be an area in the basement, a section of the garage, the corner of an attic, or the laundry room. Some of you may be comfortable with creative expression taking place in a child's room or a hallway. For some of you, it's too stressful for this process to take place in your home. If this describes you, look for classes and spaces where your children can be free to be artists, designers, builders, wrecking balls, and abominable snowmen covered in shaving cream. Be true to yourself, your children, and your home.

- Listen and pay attention to the ways your family members love to create. Which ones do your kids gravitate to? Which ones do you (and your significant other, if applicable) enjoy the most? Keep the list expansive. Allow for the joy of the activity, and soften or eliminate expectations that your child might exhibit certain skills. Some activities may be really easy for us, but our hearts don't sing when we do them, and the reverse may be true as well. This is the case with my dad, who can't carry a tune but loves to sing and often knows all the words. The joy that overtakes him trumps the off-key pitch that emanates from his voice.

- Gather the supplies you need and create the places and activities in your home that can allow for the types of creativity your family members enjoy. Over time, consider whether it's time for these creative spaces and activities to evolve to fit the current needs and preferences of family members.

- Honor the many ways creativity can be expressed and the joy that often emerges. Engage the imagination for that gold mine of possibilities. Allow joy to flourish in your home and your life. Color, doodle, paint, put together puzzles, create puzzles, scrapbook, collage, make a vision board, write, act out a play, sing silly songs, craft, cook with new ingredients, dance your own dance … The possibilities are endless.

PAINFUL TRUTHS SCREAM
FROM HIDDEN PLACES
*Releasing What's Toxic and Reclaiming Your Life*

When I have spoken of my husband to family and friends over the years, I have often acknowledged him and shared stories of his kind acts or our funny adventures. I didn't ever want to be that woman who crabbed about her husband to everyone she could. Somewhere in the process of focusing on the positive and pretending it would protect me, I lost my ability to admit when things were going wrong … and then very wrong. I buried my truths and the shadow world of our marriage even to myself until the whispers became screaming storms of almost all-day tears and fights. My fears and desperate struggle to hold together a completely unraveling situation intensified.

I have an awful *Jerry Springer* moment of tossing water from a glass right at my daughter's face after she says something cruel during a tense discussion about her graduation party preparations. I run from the house and weep on the ground in the park, amidst trees, leaves, and grass. My best friend calls me as I sit on the ground weeping. I slowly make my way back to my home, talking with her the entire time. It's late at night and I notice how cold I am. I sit on the stairs of our foyer. I blubber and weep and admit my shameful acts, how much pain I'm in, how remorseful I am.

"Open your front door, Laura," I hear her say as I clutch my phone.

I say, "What?" I feel so confused.

Again she says, almost whispering, "Open the door." I do. She walks through and holds me. I weep uncontrollably in her arms. I don't remember anyone in my whole life holding me like this, which makes me weep harder.

None of the therapists were allowed to do this. My husband had usually walked away when I'd cried. Even after I had shared that hugging or holding me when I behaved out of control would actually interrupt the pattern, he did it a handful of times, reluctantly, and then returned to the well-established disappearing act. He and most of his family of origin hated expressions of emotion. Some regularly scolded me or would do a preemptive strike of, "You aren't going to cry now, *are you?*" This had warned me to try to be somebody else and not do anything that would make them uncomfortable. I regularly failed.

It's five days away from my daughter's high school graduation party. I continue to weep and my friend continues to hold me, strong, firm, and grounded. She feels so solid, an anchor of compassion in this three-ring shit show of my life. She then takes my hand and we walk into the living room. I sit down near my husband and she guides both of us through a plan of action to get us back on track for the party. I'm relieved; I finally feel some support and a sense of clarity. Until this moment, the party had weighed heavily on my shoulders. No one in my family had been participating in any preparatory actions.

The party happens. It's a huge success and I actually have a good time. I make a point to let guests know how grateful I am for their love and friendship over the years of my daughter's growing up. Again, the darker truths remain hidden from almost everyone who attends this event.

In the weeks that follow, I hear myself saying aloud, "I think my marriage is in trouble" to a couple of my closest friends and my hair stylist of the past decade. This becomes my clue that I'm in an incredibly vulnerable place, because I never said much of anything negative about my marriage or my husband to anyone. Saying these words aloud brings the pain front and center. I can hardly breathe.

The kids know, and they avoid being in the house throughout the summer. My son leaves to be with friends on his 16th birthday to escape another horrible fight between his dad and me, and my daughter exits the home quickly, too. We had planned a delightful family celebration that my son, especially, had been anticipating. In the pain of this moment, I see the opportunity to take back my sanity, my sense of who I am. I refuse to continue to implode, though I feel strangled by my crumbling marriage. Some part of me knows it hasn't been working for a long time. It's as though I'm going through the stage of transition in the birthing cycle of my soul: one of those moments when I think I cannot go forward, but a life must be born or I will die, or so it seems.

It is in this context that I learn about a friend's 40-day challenge of exercising every day for 40 days. This intrigues me. Being an overachiever and knowing how fiercely I want to restore my sanity, I create my own 40-day challenge that consists of the following:

- I choose to exercise every day, either running or biking.

- I take a fast from the news, including from radio programs on NPR that I enjoy.

- I choose a mindfulness practice of silence. Any time I am alone, I do not turn on the radio or the TV, or even listen to music.

- I meditate at least 15 minutes a day.

- I practice feeling grateful by writing down what I am grateful for and saying "thank you" out loud for as many things as I can think of.

This becomes a powerful inner feng shui detox, my own empowering take-back-my-life cocktail. These practices become the foundation upon which a tsunami of change in every aspect of my life takes place. From this place of growing equanimity, silence, and peace, I gain clarity and see all I need to see to lift the red card over the head of my husband on the soccer field of my life and declare, "From this moment forward I will take healthy actions on my behalf and on behalf of my children." On the day my daughter moves out to begin her freshman year of college, some terrible truths about my marriage are revealed, and in the aftermath, my husband leaves our home. My gut, heart, and mind align. I know what I must do. I see the life I must save, and it is my own.

As I continue with the practices of my 40-day challenge, I begin to experience some unusual things. For the first time in my life, I hear the sound of my ring finger dabbing concealer under my eyes. It's soft, friendly. When I am with people, I really hear and feel the subtle nuance in conversations: The words that are spoken, the gestures, the feelings, and the invisible energy exchange all give me information I can use.

I notice black mold on the white wall of our bedroom closet after my soon-to-be-ex-husband removes his clothes. The outer feng shui hidden in a closet shares a powerful metaphor of his secret life and behaviors, the darkness of infidelities come to light. I realize I had been lying to myself for a long time. The black mold on the white closet wall didn't lie. I clean it thoroughly, knowing I must sell this house in the near future. *Maybe these actions will help heal him,* I think, before realizing that my words and actions cannot save another person—and anyway, it's not my job to save him.

In the midst of the peace I have cultivated, I feel energized by a force larger than myself. I begin to experience the once-elusive

"Let go and let God" thinking, which used to make me think, "Oh, come on—be real." Ideas come to me and I act on them with complete trust. My actions propel me into an unknown future, but one full of freedom, worthiness, and love. I blossom like a gorgeous lotus flower growing out of the mud. My friends notice how I lose weight and look 10 years younger. My body strengthens in tone and wakefulness. It's the most alive I have felt in years—maybe ever.

Of course, there are moments when the sweeping changes in my life catch up with me. I often wake up with a barrage of fear thoughts and anxiety coursing through my body, but engaging in the practices of my challenge allows this state to shift. The thoughts lift away like a feather nudging a bubble. Feeling present in myself—what is sometimes called an *embodied presence*—becomes more natural, easier to access. My whole being absorbs this moment, the next one, and this moment right now.

Sometimes when I am alone, I cry and scream obscenities over and over. One day for 10 minutes, I scream and cry the lyrics to "Rolling in the Deep" and "Turning Tables" by Adele while blasting her CD in my car. It's the only time I break my 40-day commitment.

Because of the silence and deep peace I cultivate on the inside, I notice things that I normally would have been too lost in chattering thoughts to see. One day I notice and watch a great blue heron silently stalk, catch, and gulp down a fish. I feel a deep calm, a deep peace in the midst of my life turning upside down and inside out. My internal world begins to shift to an oasis of calm, a shelter from the storm, and a refuge of God, silence, and strength that no one can touch.

I realize that what I have done during and since the 40-day challenge is not unlike the feng shui transformations I have made in my home: In my internal environment, I have detoxed the clutter of disempowering thoughts, embraced empowering truths, and gently released what I did not need swirling around in my mind, mostly thoughts about things I had no control over. I've been honest with myself about what matters to me and what leaves me feeling safe and supported. I've cultivated the ability to observe my surroundings, inner and outer, and make needed adjustments. In essence, I have done deep *inner* feng shui work, just as I have done deep feng shui work in my home, and have begun to reclaim my life.

Here are some ideas to consider when your life happens to be imploding:

- Pursue some form of seeking silence. Finding quiet in a noisy world may restore you to a sanity you did not know was possible. The simple act of turning off all the external noise can be a powerful first step. You may then notice how noisy and painful it is inside your inner world. At this point, seeking deep internal peace may become your desire. There are many pathways to this. Choose one that resonates with you.

- Exercise is known to have many, many benefits. Our bodies were designed for movement. Consider some form of movement such as dancing, walking, doing yoga, stretching, hula hooping, biking, or swimming. Change it up if this inspires you. Just move.

- Self-care often is a contribution to others. Deep self-care physically, emotionally, mentally, and spiritually fuels the life force within us. Just as you plug a phone into the electrical socket to charge it, our bodies and minds need to be recharged and cared for deeply to work effectively, especially during times of intense challenges.

- While you may not need or want to take on a full buffet of self-care practices, it will make a positive difference to choose one and stick with it for as long as you can. Make it a game for your own transformation. Maybe let one person very close to you (or a group of friends) know so they can cheer you on, or keep it to yourself if that would better motivate you.

- Feel your feelings, as they will mostly likely crash around you in waves. Consider that emotions are energy in motion, and the more they move through you the clearer and freer you will be. Attempt to do so in ways that are safe and that fit your way of feeling and expressing your strong emotions. Seek support if needed.

## A TSUNAMI OF CHANGE

*Asking Yourself "Who Am I and What Now?"*
*when Life Implodes*

The double release of my daughter to college and my 22-year-old marriage frees me to pursue deeper dreams and cracks me wide open. *Embrace change,* says the feng shui consultant inside of me at the same time as every cell of my being cries and screams through this tsunami of upheaval. I grieve the loss of my old life even if certain facets of it seemed, at times, like a numb prison of unworthiness.

I'm experiencing a spiritual lift-off, like a rocket ship whose booster falls away into the blackness with no oxygen. Grateful to be carried this high but now seemingly lost in space, I flounder and find a new gravitational pull. It leaves me breathless, on my knees, in complete awe and terror. My higher self and my terrified self work double shifts to face nurses and staff during my son's ten-day hospitalization, with one attorney (whom I didn't hire) who stirred up fear and anger in an attempt to line her own pockets, and with an entire household to manage while flying solo and worrying constantly about my unclear future.

I rake, blow, and bag leaves. I let the dogs out and in, feed them, feed my boy and me, wash the dishes, meet with a realtor and discuss selling the house, update my resume, and continue sleeping on my side of a king-size bed. My small self has moments of sadness, anger, and despair. I have yet to feel lonely, however. I realize that I felt lonely, frustrated, and unloved inside the marriage, and I feel none of these now. I continue what I think of as "inner feng shui rituals": actions to create maximum serenity, such as running, walking the dogs, meditating, and writing down things I am grateful for. I suspend these rituals briefly when I work a 51-hour week, grateful for the temporary professional job and setting.

I feel full and alive. Strength grows from deep inside of me. This serves me at 5 a.m. New Year's morning, as I face teen boys in our family room reeking of alcohol, a girl in the bathroom I do not know, and later the discovery of egg yolk hardened in yellow streaks on the stucco sides and front of my house. None of this looks or feels like something a feng shui consultant is supposed to live through and yet I do. I remain humbled by all of it. I know I must stay inside the eye of these storms and mostly run like the buffalo straight into them. Avoidance isn't really an option here. Managing so much chaos allows little time for me to consider grief, loss, or hiding under the covers. Exhaustion seems like something I place in a deep storage locker. It doesn't even register.

Courage fuels me like dark chocolates that I cannot stop eating. It's not that I don't feel the fear; it's that I'm focused on more important issues: my son's life and health, a full sense of freedom and worthiness, the search for a new home, and the creation of financial independence. My little self can no longer be in charge; it never really was. Upon realizing this, I experience a full surrender, a complete *let go*. I allow this higher energy to guide me. My gut becomes my compass, my heart a warrior and a weeping bundle of loss, and my mind both a channel of inspired thoughts that I act upon and a holding tank of the traumas I lived. I hold a vision of all I can become as a woman and a truth teller rising broken-hearted and brave from the darkest times of my adult life. Inside the fire of all these traumas I find an awakened self, vibrant and alive. I live broken open and breaking free.

Here are ideas to support you in your own times of challenge and change:

- Get serious about clearing away all belongings you no longer need, never loved, or feel indifferent about. Create room for the life and experiences you desire now. If not now, when? Start where the clutter agitates you the most.

- If needed, bring closure and completion to unhealthy relationships or relationships you've outgrown with grace, dignity, and strong, solid boundaries. Live true to yourself and who you are now.

- Begin to know in your bones that you are lovable, worthy, and powerful beyond measure.

- Engage practices that support your healthiest self, such as smiling, yoga, deep breathing, laughing, listening to music you love, and taking a news fast.

- Exercise, meditate, and feel grateful. All three of these are now scientifically proven to increase the experience of happiness and fulfillment in life. These three activities prove to be gateways to happiness. In one study, results showed that feeling gratitude for two and a half minutes every day for 21 days shifted even the grumpiest people in the direction of happiness.

- Spend time with friends and family members who love and respect you. They mean the world in times of challenge and change.

GOODBYE HOUSE, GOODBYE MARRIAGE
*Reflecting on Profound Life Transitions*

Most children go through a phase of emotional meltdowns, which some experts refer to as *disequilibrium*, right before a new developmental stage comes. I've been living through disequilibrium for eight months now. You may have experienced this sense of being out of sorts during times of major life transitions. It's an out-of-control and disorienting feeling, filled with the realization that you are not the puppeteer and maybe you never were. Yet this feeling also signals being on the brink of a breakthrough in being fully alive and at peace.

I drive into the garage of the home that is now listed for sale. I look up and see a large diagonal crack on the ceiling in what is considered the love corner in feng shui, which holds that certain areas of our home correspond to domains of our lives. In my feng shui consulting and my own life, I often see issues reflected in our lives and in the corresponding areas of our homes. The house still knows. The crack remains as the only outward symbol of the divorce; all the other external reminders have been healed.

Cleaning and painting have made the mold in the love corner of the basement disappear. The once-moldy closet of the main bedroom was cleaned six months ago and remains pristine white, its integrity restored. The other clues the house whispered lived in the upstairs bathroom, the self-awareness domain. The sink, which had been clogged for months, now drains water freely with new pipes installed; a new mirror covers the tile gap where a medicine cabinet used to be; and a new towel bar installed with beautiful ceramic holders fills the holes we showered with for 10 years. In ways both hidden and obvious to the naked eye, the house has spoken powerful truths about healing, restoration, and fresh beginnings.

The house looks and feels ready for its future as I work rigorously for weeks, in short and long bursts, deep-cleaning and staging it. A trustworthy trio of hard-working men clean carpeting, repair, restore, and paint with quality, care, and vision. I'm grateful for their support. The process allows me to begin to move toward closure with a home I love.

Amid all the hard work, I mostly keep in lockdown my sadness and grief over the loss of a marriage I'd fought for and a home I had helped transform. At times, though, the grief spills out, such as the day when I call Cindy, the woman who grooms and boards my dogs, to ask if she can temporarily care for them until my move is complete. One of the dogs is really sick. I can no longer clean the pee and poo in the sick dog's crate and off the floor every single morning and throughout the day while readying the home for visits from potential buyers. In my conversation with Cindy, I feel safe enough to openly weep.

On another bright sunny spring morning when I must leave the house early for appraisers who are coming, I pull out of the driveway and completely break down. I sob as I drive away from this house I love, not certain where I am going. I see a favorite coffee shop and pull into the drive-through, to be greeted by a large screen with a young man smiling at me. "Welcome! What can I get started for you?" I order my chai latte. "How's your day going?" he asks.

I begin to cry again and blubber that I'm selling a home I

love. "Well, I guess all good things must come to an end," he responds. Yes.

I drive around to the pick-up window and hand the cashier a gift card. She says, "John's got this." I think she means that he's the one who has to take my card, so I wait a bit and then extend my card once again. When she hands me my beverage, she explains, "John paid for your tea." This, of course, makes me cry harder and choke out a thank-you. This simple act of kindness by a stranger takes me to a whole other place of weeping, with grief now mixed with gratitude.

After that day, I begin to move toward equilibrium again with a new sense of resolve. I feel strong and calm enough to reflect on the broken relationship that was supposed to be the foundation of our family. I see clearly the bankrupt patterns of communication with my soon-to-be ex-husband. I now know the difference between love and abuse and how they can dance together; how love can morph into manipulation. When addiction takes over, blaming and shaming run the entire show, and self-responsibility escapes out the back door. But I too am responsible: I lied to myself for years, and I betrayed my highest and best self. This truth lives as the most profound lesson. I now live worthy of respect, kindness, and love.

As I rake leaves in the back of the house for what I know will be the last time, flashes of memories dance in my mind. Playing four square and around the world on the concrete pad … watching my children squeal with delight on the play equipment … playing volleyball and badminton with friends, with a net hung between the two large oak trees…and scrambling to catch one guinea pig waddling loose in the bushes by the fence.

Mostly past the earlier disequilibrium, I feel gratitude and peace about the house I am leaving. The house and I healed and transformed together. This house will forever be the place where I fulfilled a dream of mothering. Now, like a wise mother bird, this house gently nudges me out of her nest, trusting that I will soar.

Here are some tips you may consider during times of transition and grateful goodbyes:

- Repair what annoys and agitates you the most in your home within the next month. Enjoy the benefits of things working properly in your home. Notice how these repairs translate to your *life* working more smoothly and with greater ease. With the agitation gone, we can focus energy on experiences we desire with the people we love.

- Consider "Loving what is" as a way of living your life. Practicing deep acceptance of reality can free you to be at peace, especially in times of transition, upheaval, and the stormy seas of life. Divorce happens. Moving happens. Other losses, expected and unexpected, happen. Breathing through the surrender brings clarity. As Byron Katie says, "When we stop opposing reality, action becomes simple, fluid, kind, and fearless."

- Take simple actions each day aligned with a clear vision and purpose. For example, I created the vision of "single, happy, and free." Include nurturing self-care activities such as exercise you love, meditation, and belly laughing. Call friends who love you. Respond to what is right in front of you. That's all you can do sometimes, and it is the healthiest choice.

- Expect every single day to be entirely different than the one before, and allow yourself to have periods of disequilibrium. Emotions are best felt fully and thoroughly, even the uncomfortable ones. They serve a purpose and often propel us forward. This is the nature of profound transitions. I know that at first it feels like quicksand. Feelings of grief may take you to your knees. Know that life supports you. You are powerful beyond measure, even as your heart breaks wide open. You can take action and cry at the same time.

- Allow relationships that have run their course the dignity of release. Free yourself. Free others to live their lives unbounded by your judgments of their choices. Focus on loving yourself and living true to who you are and what you are creating. Consider staying focused on the business of your life, of your belongings, of who you are becoming. Your precious life deserves that attention, kindness, and care.

## THE COURAGE TO LET GO
*Embracing the Bitter and the Sweet*

Letting go takes courage and strength. It's sometimes easy, mostly difficult, and often scary. At times it is a relief, but at other times it can be draining. When letting go becomes a conscious choice that you do not avoid, it can be deeply liberating. In the process of letting go, something else must emerge. That something is often an enduring sense of freedom.

The past several months have provided doctorate-level training in letting go. I let go of a marriage. I let go of my daughter when she began college. I let go of a house I loved, along with many belongings and beloved treasures from that house. I let go of a piano, an elliptical exercise machine, books, décor, artwork, DVDs, CDs, clothing, games, puzzles, and jewelry. I let go of bird feeders, wind chimes, large outdoor pots for plants, and bookshelves.

I let go of all my ex's relatives, almost 60 people total. I loved and felt close to many of them; they are that kind of family. It seemed like many of them loved me, but none of them has reached out to build a bridge. Though it was not my choice, they live dead to me now. A month ago I let go of a friend who passed away after surrendering to cancer that took her body but not her gentle spirit; she was two weeks away from her 50th birthday. With all these relationships, I grieve inside the silence of their absence. The grief comes in unpredictable waves that I allow to flow through me, the tears running rapidly down my face as I breathe through all this loss.

I let go and let a higher force lift me. Something trans-
forms deep inside of me as I surrender my small self and all
the lies I have believed, some for only a few years and some
since I was a child. I set them free. I surrender to feeling peace
and joy. My friends hold my hand and hug me, and I am held
and loved by life. I'm not certain of the turning point when
this full-on surrender happens, but it does, and it seems there
is no turning back from this new place of clarity and trust.

Now sitting at my dining room table, where I eat and work,
I see belongings that continue to inspire me. Despite releasing
so many possessions I enjoyed and the home that held them,
I'm filled with gratitude for all I have, for all that I am. I have
fallen deeply in love with my life. I'm unrecognizable to myself.
I'm single, happy, broken-open, and free.

The initial 40-day challenge that I undertook when my life im-
ploded, which I'd hoped would support me to face difficulties with
equanimity, has grown into my mandatory self-care package and
a way of living my life. These practices serve as a reminder of the
good that has arisen amid the loss, and they help me find the spiritual strength to be joyful, eager, clear, and fully awake and alive.

It seems that living through the intense storms of the past
10 months has washed away many remnants of my troubled
past. I release what I don't want to take forward into my new
life. I finally stop struggling and fighting with my life, with
myself. Quite simply, I let go.

Here are some ideas for cultivating the courage to let go
and live true to your dreams:

- Contemplate your deepest desires. Maybe you want to
  downsize, declutter, or let go of relationships or activities

that drain your life energy. Maybe you want to travel, create a new career, or spend quality time with people you love. Imagine your life without fear. What would you be doing with your time, with your days?

- Consider doing that one thing that you've resisted doing but that you sense might ultimately help you. Taking this action may involve letting go of fear or feeling the fear and doing it anyway.

- Gently open one drawer or one closet in your home or office. Look and see what is actually staring at you. Ask yourself: *Do I love this?* If the answer is no, let it go. If the answer is yes, keep the item and take a moment to be grateful for its presence in your life. If the answer is maybe, then keep it until you are clear about whether it gets to be part of your life going forward.

- Consider having honest and open conversations with the people with whom you struggle the most—or at least fair but honest conversations with yourself about these difficult relationships. Look for places to let go and for places to hold on, if there are any. Muster the courage to walk away from those who would break your spirit or are breaking your heart. Though difficult, it can be done. Your life spirit and freedom are worth it.

## A Grateful Heart: Acknowledgments

To all my clients and students: You open your homes and lives to me, and remain receptive to this body of wisdom and to my help. I'm grateful to you for sharing your challenges, dreams, heartaches, and heartwarming stories of home transformation and inspired living. Thank you for running with the ideas we discuss to create your very own feng shui expression. Your actions inspire me deeply. It continues to be a privilege and honor to work with all of you.

To Terah Kathryn Collins, Liv Kellgren, Becky Iott, Karen Abler Carrasco, and all the alums of the Western School of Feng Shui: You are my soul sisters who blaze trails all around me and who have ushered me into this amazing, powerful, transformative world of feng shui. I am forever grateful.

To Wayne Dyer, Martha Beck, Elizabeth Gilbert, Cheryl Strayed, Louise Hay, Alan Cohen, Sonia Choquette, Brene Brown, Eckert Tolle, Esther Hicks, Oprah Winfrey, Pat Conroy, Rhonda Byrne, and Karen Kingston: All your words deeply and profoundly inspire my evolution as a spiritual being having a human experience and the burning desire to share my stories and voice with the world. Because of all of you, I freely, fearlessly, and passionately share my truth.

To Nita Sweeney: Thank you for encouraging and inspiring me to write from my soul and to run long distances.

To Janice Berry Paganini, my cherished friend and gifted, honest editor: Thank you for keeping me true to my voice, heart, and wisdom by way of your own clear voice, kind heart, and brilliance.

To Kim Dhuyvetter: Thank you for the beautiful cover design.

To Mark Levine and the Mill City Press team: Thank you for your publishing wisdom, kindness, and support.

To L.: Thank you for your vivaciousness, wisdom, coaching, and fierce stand for me living a life I love powerfully and fearlessly. This book and the life I have now would not have happened without you. You have been the wind beneath my wings, and the arms that have held me strong.

To Teresa DeVitt: Thank you for inspiring my self-care practices, writing at the library with me, consistently encouraging me to be an inspired soul living my dreams awake, and being a sparkling, life-giving friend.

To H.: Thank you for being my second greatest spiritual teacher. From you I learned to see fully my own heart, beauty, and worthiness. Because of you, I leaped forward and found grace, strength, resilience, and fearlessness.

To Cathy Davis, Barb Marshall, Ann Joyce, Kristen Peairs, Kathy Shipley, Mary Ware, Alison Hazelbaker, Susie Kalyn, Vanessa Bey, Deb Bowe, Stephanie Jursek, Kay Knox, Julie Quackenbush, Sharron Kulp, Emma Welsh-Huggins, Michelle Reese, Jim Cowan, Michael Hernley, Terry Olive, Tom Thon, Ken Lazar, Jeff Young, Chris B'orja, Tom Wentz, and all my friends at Tuesday Tune-up: Thank you for believing in me and consistently cheering for me to succeed and to live true to myself.

To Doug Grossman: Thank you for your listening, friendship, compassion, and laughter, and for gifting me the phrase "crazy beautiful life"!

To Don Fortner: Thank you for the years of friendship, your unwavering belief in me, your support for my meditation practice and my creative expression, and your unconditional love. Thank you, also, for the page layout of this book.

To Tom Giere: Thank you for your whole-hearted acceptance, kindness, care, support, and friendship, and for the pure joy you bring to my life. You are a treasure.

For my parents: I am grateful to you for giving me life so I could honor this gift by creating a beautiful one, and for our miraculous reconciliation and forever love, sweetness, and tenderness. Thank you for believing in me and for loving me my whole life as best as you knew how.

For Julianna and Matthew: Thank you for allowing me to live my passion for parenting and create amazing, life-affirming relationships with both of you. Being your mom is the *best* thing I've ever done with my life. I love you both, forever and always.

CPSIA information can be obtained
at www.ICGtesting.com
Printed in the USA
BVOW06s2158120117
473394BV00014B/125/P